Contents

W9-BZO-230

FOOD GAMES

FOOD EXPERIMENTS

FOOD SERVICE PROJECTS

Food Fun™

DEVOTIONS FOR CHILDREN'S MINISTRY

by
Dennis and Lana Jo McLaughlin

Group
Loveland, Colorado

Dedication

To our children, Layton, Austin, and Karlie, who are each a daily reminder of how wonderfully God has blessed us.

FoodFun™: Devotions for Children's Ministry
Copyright © 1999 Group Publishing, Inc.

All rights reserved. No part of this book may be reproduced in any manner whatsoever without prior written permission from the publisher, except where noted in the text and in the case of brief quotations embodied in critical articles and reviews. For information write Permissions, Group Publishing, Inc., Dept. PD, P.O. Box 481, Loveland, CO 80539.

Visit our Web site: **www.grouppublishing.com**

Credits
Authors: Dennis and Lana Jo McLaughlin
Editors: Lori Haynes Niles and Amy Nappa
Creative Development Editor: Dave Thornton
Chief Creative Officer: Joani Schultz
Copy Editor: Shirley Michaels
Art Director: Jean Bruns
Computer Graphic Artist: Fred Schuth
Illustrator: Viki Woodworth
Production Manager: Peggy Naylor
Cover Art Director: Jeff A. Storm
Cover Designer: Cukjaki Design
Cover Photographer: Don Jones

Unless otherwise noted, Scripture taken from the HOLY BIBLE, NEW INTERNATIONAL VERSION. Copyright © 1973, 1978, 1984 by International Bible Society. Used by permission of Zondervan Publishing House. All rights reserved.

Library of Congress Cataloging-in-Publication Data

McLaughlin, Dennis R.
    Food fun devotions for children's ministry/by Dennis and Lana Jo McLaughlin.
        p.   cm.
    Includes indexes.
    ISBN 0-7644-2081-X (alk. paper)
    1. Bible--Study and teaching (Elementary)--Activity programs. 2. Christian education of children. 3. Snack foods.
    I. McLaughlin, Lana Jo. II. Title.
BS618.M45   1999
268'.432--DC21   99-29456
                                                           CIP

10 9 8 7 6 5 4 3   08 07 06 05 04 03 02
Printed in the United States of America.

Introduction

"Give your children a fish, and you'll feed them for a day. Teach them how to fish, and you'll feed them for a lifetime."

You've probably heard this bit of wisdom, most likely in relationship to feeding people in impoverished countries. But what does it have to do with Christian education? How does this saying relate to the spiritual needs of children? The answer is clear. Of primary importance in Christian education is helping children learn to make solid Christian decisions for their lives. This means we don't merely give them answers for their immediate concerns, but we teach them to apply God's truths to their lives themselves.

The people of the Old Testament were successful in this regard, primarily because of their efforts at making religious education life-oriented rather than just information-oriented. The Hebrew people used everyday life experiences to teach their children about God. The Bible places great emphasis on teaching faith to our children in this way. If we want our children to follow God, we must make God part of their everyday experiences (Deuteronomy 6:6-9).

If you were to do an in-depth analysis of teaching methods employed throughout the Bible, you'd discover that biblical teachers emphasized learning rather than teaching. Jesus, for one, never hesitated to use life experience as a basis for teaching. He understood that people learn the most when they're able to relate their lessons to everyday life experiences.

Unfortunately, Christian teachers today have fallen short of capitalizing on teaching that engages all the learner's senses. In *The Second Coming of the Church*, George Barna, prolific Christian author and researcher, makes a convincing case that even though people today are desperately searching for spiritual truth, Christian churches are not providing the answers they need. Sadly, many Christian education programs are more interested in filling an hour's time with busy work than in providing children with a true learning environment.

We must guard against this. Whenever we have opportunities within the church to teach children, we have to do our best to give them experiences from which they can learn to make life-changing decisions. *FoodFun™: Devotions for Children's Ministry* was written with that goal in mind. Each activity was designed specifically to maximize learning experiences for elementary school children.

Kids keep telling us that one of their favorite activities at church is making snacks. So in the interest of capitalizing on their interest, we developed more than forty Bible-intensive, snack-based lessons. These lessons are designed to help kids either create a snack that reinforces a Bible truth or use food as an object lesson to emphasize a point.

The activities have been divided into five lesson categories: Food Crafts, Food Devotions, Food Games, Food Experiments, and Food Service Projects. The activities can be used during snack time in worship, in almost any classroom setting, at after-school outreach programs, sports programs, or parties. You'll be pleased at the fun the kids will have and, even more, amazed at how much they'll learn.

Each activity can be used with multi-age levels, from kindergarten through fifth grade. We've also been pleasantly surprised at how many teenagers and adults enjoy these activities. Each one can be used as an entire lesson in itself or as part of a longer lesson. The activities are flexible and can be adapted to meet the needs of your group.

HOW TO USE THIS BOOK

You'll notice each easy-to-use activity is based on a particular theme and a specific Bible passage. In addition, each one has several at-a-glance references.

• **Cook's Eye View** provides a quick overview of the activity and lesson.

• **Stuff 'n' Fixin's** identifies all the supplies you'll need.

• **Gettin' Ready** lets you know what you'll need to prepare before the children arrive.

• **Mixin' 'n' Movin'** is where the activity actually begins. This section will walk you step-by-step through the lesson.

• **Bringin' It to a Boil** is discussion-oriented and helps children apply the lesson to real-life situations.

• **Turnin' Up the Heat** is an optional question or thought to dig deeper into the meaning of each activity.

• **Sharin' It With Someone** challenges kids to apply the lesson to their lives.

SAFETY AND OTHER HELPFUL HINTS

• Since all activities are food-related, make an effort to use sanitary health practices. Be sure utensils and work areas are clean, and ask kids to wash their hands before and after each activity.

• Provide close supervision when using an oven. Allow adults only to handle the "hot stuff."

• When a sharp knife is required, do the cutting yourself.

• Obviously, the younger the children, the more help and supervision they'll need. Consider using a helper, such as another adult or a responsible teenager, when working with small children.

• A few of the activities call for kids to form small groups. This interactive learning method is especially effective for large classes. For small classes, the lesson is equally effective by having the kids stay together in one group. Remember, each activity is adaptable to the needs of your group.

• The lessons are based on the New International Version Bible translation. While a Bible for the teacher is not listed as an "ingredient" for each activity, it is assumed you'll have one nearby.

• Finally, take pictures to make a lasting record of these experiences. You can put the photos into a scrapbook, decorate a bulletin board with them, or send them home for kids and parents to enjoy.

A FINAL NOTE

We hope you're ready to jump right in and use these activities. However, they're merely tools. You are the real gift given to the children. Your work is invaluable. And if ever for a moment you forget why you're doing it, remember—"you're feeding them for a lifetime."

Grace and peace,

Dennis and Lana McLaughlin

Creatin' Heaven and Earth

SCRIPTURE

Genesis 1:1

COOK'S EYE VIEW: Each child will create an earth out of popcorn. Afterward they'll discuss their role in taking care of both the earth and the people of the earth.

STUFF 'N' FIXIN'S: (For every 7 popcorn "earths") 2 bags microwave popcorn, ¼ cup butter, a 10-ounce package large marshmallows or 4 cups small marshmallows, cooking oil spray. several large bowls, a mixing utensil, a microwave oven, blue and green food coloring, and plastic wrap.

GETTIN' READY: If you want to save time, pop the popcorn before children arrive. Arrange the items so kids can reach them easily and participate in the project. If your group is young and you think they may have difficulty finding a Bible passage, write each of the following verses on an index card: Genesis 22:18; Psalm 24:1; Matthew 6:10; Luke 2:14; and Revelation 21:1.

MIXIN' 'N' MOVIN'

Begin by reading aloud or having one of the kids read aloud Genesis 1:1. Ask:

• **What would it have been like to have watched God create the earth?**

• **What's your favorite part of God's creation?**

Tell kids they're each going to create an earth out of popcorn. If you haven't already done so, pop the microwave popcorn according to the directions on the bag. Next, heat one-quarter cup of butter and a ten-ounce package of marshmallows together in the microwave for approximately two minutes or until they're melted. Be sure to check the mixture after one minute and stir. (If you are using food coloring, separate the marshmallow mixture into two batches; add green food coloring to one batch and blue to the other.) Coat the inside of a large bowl with cooking oil spray, add popcorn, pour the melted marshmallows over it and mix thoroughly. Use blue and green food coloring to prepare one bowl of blue popcorn and one bowl of green.

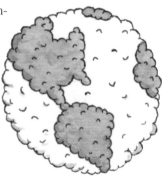

Have each child spray his or her hands lightly with cooking oil. (This will help keep the popcorn from sticking.) Then have children each take a handful of the popcorn and marshmallow mixture and form it into a ball to make the earth. Allow kids to take a bit of each color to sculpt the land and oceans of the earth.

Tear sheets of plastic wrap off the roll, and lightly spray cooking oil on one side of each piece. Have the kids wrap their newly created earths in the pieces of plastic wrap and save them to enjoy after the discussion.

BRINGIN' IT TO A BOIL

Divide your class into five groups, and assign each group one of the Scriptures listed under the Gettin' Ready instructions. Have them locate each Scripture, read it aloud in the group, and then discuss what it has to do with the earth. After approximately five minutes, call everyone together, and ask a member of each group to read its Bible verse to the class. Have someone else in the group tell what the group thought it meant.

If your class members are too young to accomplish this on their own, keep them together as a group. Read each Bible verse out loud, and ask children to tell you what they think each verse has to do with the earth. Continue the discussion by asking the following questions:

- **What does it mean to be blessed?**
- **How are we blessed to be part of God's earth?**
- **If the earth belongs to the Lord, how should we treat it?**
- **What kinds of things can people do to make the earth a better place?**
- **What can we do as Christians to help keep peace on earth?**

TURNIN' UP THE HEAT

What is one thing you can personally do to make the earth a better place to live?

SHARIN' IT WITH SOMEONE

Think of one thing you and your family can do together to make the world a better place in which to live—for example, pick up trash in a nearby park, begin recycling, or build a bird feeder. When you get home, invite your family to help you with this project so the world will be a better place in which to live.

Friendship Snowflakes

SCRIPTURE
Job 6:14-17

COOK'S EYE VIEW: Kids will make snowflakes out of tortillas. They will discuss how Job's friends were undependable, like melting snowflakes, and will learn the importance of being dependable friends.

STUFF 'N' FIXIN'S: Large round flour tortillas (1 for each child), butter, cinnamon, sugar, plastic knives, scissors (1 pair for each child), tortilla keeper or microwave-safe covered dish, microwave oven, empty salt shaker, and embroidery floss (optional).

GETTIN' READY: Before kids arrive, wash each pair of scissors since they will be used to cut tortillas. Warm the tortillas in the microwave, and put them into a tortilla keeper or other covered dish to help them stay warm. (The tortillas must be warm and pliable for this activity to work properly.) Mix cinnamon and sugar together in a shaker. Set out the items on a clean table where the kids will have plenty of room to work.

MIXIN' 'N' MOVIN'

Say: **There's a man in the Bible named Job. A lot of bad things happened to Job. His animals were stolen, and some of them were killed. His children all died in an accident. Then Job became sick and his whole body was covered with sores that really hurt! He had three friends who he thought he could depend on to help him during these troubled times. But his friends were no help at all. Listen as I read a Scripture that tells what Job had to say about his friends.**

Read Job 6:14-17 aloud. Say: **Job said his friends were like melting snow.**

Ask:

• **Why is snow undependable?**

• **What do you think Job meant by saying his friends were like melting snow?**

• **Do you have any friends who are like melting snow? If so, tell what makes them that way.**

Say: **As we're thinking about friends, we're going to make some tasty friendship snowflakes out of tortillas. Gather around the table. Take a warm tortilla and fold it in half. Then fold it again. Use scissors to cut small pieces out of the tortilla to make a snowflake. Watch as I demonstrate how to do it.** (Refer to the diagram on p. 11.)

Have the kids unfold their tortillas to see the beautiful snowflakes they've created. Instruct the kids to put a light coat of butter on the snowflakes and sprinkle them with sugar and cinnamon.

BRINGIN' IT TO A BOIL

Say: **Let's eat our snowflakes to show how snow is undependable, as Job's friends were.** As the kids are enjoying their snack, ask:

• **What makes a friend undependable?**
• **What makes a friend dependable?**
• **Tell about a special friend you have and what makes him or her dependable.**

TURNIN' UP THE HEAT

What things can you do to show others you're a good friend?

SHARIN' IT WITH SOMEONE

Make a friendship bracelet by braiding colored embroidery floss. To begin, take three strands of embroidery floss, and tie a knot in one end. Then braid the floss, and tie a knot in the other end. Leave enough string on each end so the bracelet can be tied on someone's wrist or ankle. Give it to one of your favorite friends this week to thank him or her for being a good friend.

Buildin' a Church

SCRIPTURE
I Corinthians
16:19

COOK'S EYE VIEW: Kids will each construct an edible church out of graham crackers and frosting. After they have finished their creations, the kids will expand their understanding of the word and meaning of church.

STUFF 'N' FIXIN'S: Graham crackers, canned frosting, plastic knives (1 for each participant), paper to cover and protect the tables, paper plates (sturdy ones work best), and paper towels or damp cloths.

GETTIN' READY: Before the kids arrive, cover the tables with paper for easy cleanup. Place the ingredients around the table, making sure there's adequate room for each participant to work. If you have a large number of students, divide the frosting into several small bowls.

MIXIN' 'N' MOVIN'

Have each child find a partner and take a few minutes to share one thing he or she likes about church. After a couple of minutes, give a signal for the children to stop talking. Have the kids stay in their pairs, and ask each child to tell what his or her partner shared. If you have a large group, call on only a few children instead of allowing each person to share.

Say: **Now tell your partner what you think is the most important part of church. For example, is it a place in the church? Is it the time we listen to the pastor? Is it the worship or singing time? Or do you have another idea?**

Give kids a few minutes, and then have them share their thoughts with the whole class. (You might consider writing their ideas on a chalkboard or dry-erase board so everyone can see all the creative answers.)

Say: **We're going to talk more about the most important part of a church in a little while, so let's remember what we've shared here. Now, let's work on a fun activity together.**

Have everyone gather around the tables. Give the children each a paper plate to place their creations on.

Say: **We're each going to build a church using graham crackers and frosting. As you make your building, be creative and have fun!**

Help the kids spread frosting along the edges of the crackers, and demonstrate how to place cracker pieces together to make a building. Encourage the kids to decorate their churches with walkways, steeples, and other additions. Afterward, give the kids an opportunity to admire one another's creations.

BRINGIN' IT TO A BOIL

After the kids have had an opportunity to wash any frosting from their hands, have them stand in a circle. Explain that you're going to ask them to make some choices and they're to respond according to your instructions. (After each question, have the kids return to the circle.) Say:

• **Those who think the building is the most important part of the church, stand in the middle of the circle.**

• **Those who think the people are the most important part of the church, move to the middle of the circle.**

• **Those who think it doesn't matter where people meet to have church as long as they worship, praise, and learn about Jesus, move to the middle of the circle.**

Have the kids sit down and begin eating their church creations as you read them 1 Corinthians 16:19. Ask:

• **What's unusual about the place where Aquila and Priscilla met for church?**

• **Why would their church have been meeting in a home?**

• **How do you think the people of your church would react if your church building burned down or if it was blown over by a strong wind? What would they do? Where would they meet?**

TURNIN' UP THE HEAT

Do you think it's better for a church to meet in a home, a school, or a traditional church building? Explain your answer.

SHARIN' IT WITH SOMEONE

Think of someone who doesn't go to church. This week tell that person what's special about your church, and invite him or her to come and visit.

Boats in a Storm

SCRIPTURE

Mark 4:35-40

COOK'S EYE VIEW: Kids will make boats from hard-boiled eggs and discuss the disciple's fear when they were in a boat during a storm. They will learn how to rely on Jesus during the storms (hard times) in their lives.

STUFF 'N' FIXIN'S: Hard-boiled eggs (1 for each child), 5 or 6 extra hard-boiled eggs, sliced American cheese (1 slice for every 3 kids), toothpicks, mayonnaise, mustard, vinegar, salt, pepper, jelly beans, a medium-sized bowl, plastic knives, spoons, re-sealable plastic sandwich bags, photocopies of the "Jesus Jelly Bean Prayer" handout (p. 15), and crayons or markers.

GETTIN' READY: Practice making a boat so you can easily demonstrate it for the kids. Begin by peeling the shell from a hard-boiled egg. Cut the egg in half lengthwise, and scoop the yoke into a bowl for later use. Cut two cheese triangles, each approximately one-half inch in height. Put a toothpick between the two slices, and gently squeeze them together. Put the cheese sail into the edge of the egg half. (See diagram.)

 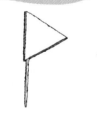 

MIXIN' 'N' MOVIN'

Begin by reading Mark 4:35-40 to the kids. Ask:
- **Have you ever been caught in a storm? If so, tell about it.**
- **What do most people do when they're caught in a storm?**
- **What did the disciples do when they were caught in a storm?**

Say: **Today we're going to make boats to remind us of the one Jesus and the disciples were in when the storm came. Gather around the table as I demonstrate how to make a boat out of a hard-boiled egg.** (Refer to the earlier instructions and diagram.)

As the kids remove the egg yolks, place all the yolks in a bowl. Mix them with mayonnaise, mustard, vinegar, and salt and pepper to taste. Have the kids spoon some of the mixture into their egg "boats."

Then say: **Now take a jelly bean, and put it into your boat to represent Jesus.**

BRINGIN' IT TO A BOIL

As the kids are enjoying their snacks, say: **Jesus and his disciples were out in a boat during a storm. We've all seen a rain or snow storm, but there are other kinds of storms we have in our lives also. For example, when people say they have a storm in their lives, they mean they're going through a difficult situation.** Ask:

- **What kinds of storms can people have in their lives?**
- **After hearing the story about the disciples in the boat, what can we do when we're going through a storm in our lives?**
- **Tell about the memory of a storm in your life when you trusted Jesus. What happened when you trusted Jesus?**

Hand out a copy of the "Jesus Jelly Bean Prayer" below to each child. Have the kids follow along as you read it aloud.

Say: **This prayer is not for you to keep but to give to someone you know who's going through a storm in his or her life.**

Give each child a resealable plastic bag. Have kids put a small handful of jelly beans into their bags. (Be sure there is one of each color.) Then have kids color the jelly bean border on the prayer handout and put this in the bag, too.

TURNIN' UP THE HEAT

What can you do to help a friend who is going through a storm in his or her life?

SHARIN' IT WITH SOMEONE

Find someone to give your bag and "Jesus Jelly Bean Prayer" to.

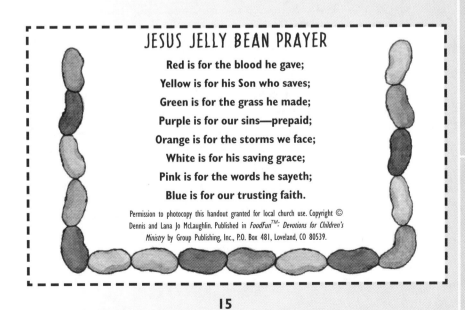

JESUS JELLY BEAN PRAYER

Red is for the blood he gave;
Yellow is for his Son who saves;
Green is for the grass he made;
Purple is for our sins—prepaid;
Orange is for the storms we face;
White is for his saving grace;
Pink is for the words he sayeth;
Blue is for our trusting faith.

Permission to photocopy this handout granted for local church use. Copyright © Dennis and Lana Jo McLaughlin. Published in *FoodFun*™*: Devotions for Children's Ministry* by Group Publishing, Inc., P.O. Box 481, Loveland, CO 80539.

Sleepin' in Graham Comfort

SCRIPTURE

Psalm 4:8 and
Psalm 63:6

COOK'S EYE VIEW: Kids will use frosting to decorate graham crackers to look like kids in sleeping bags. Discussion will center on overcoming fears about night and darkness because God watches over us even when we sleep.

STUFF 'N' FIXIN'S: Graham crackers, frosting, food coloring, cake decorating tubes with various tips (1 for every 4 or 5 kids), table or plastic knives, several small bowls, mixing spoons, pieces of paper or index cards, pencils, and enlarged copy of diagram on page 17.

GETTIN' READY: Prepare various colors of frosting in the small bowls by mixing it with food coloring. Place all the snack supplies on a table with plenty of room for kids to work.

MIXIN' 'N' MOVIN'

Begin by allowing kids to share stories about when they've been camping or when they've slept in a tent. Follow their stories by asking these questions:

- **What did you like best about camping or sleeping outside?**
- **What did you like least about it?**
- **Have you ever had a scary experience while camping? If so, tell us about it.**

Say: **It can be scary to sleep out in a tent at night, especially if you're by yourself. Even when we are sleeping in our own beds at night, sometimes we can get scared, especially after we've had a bad dream.** (You might ask for a show of hands from kids who've had scary dreams.)

Say: **We're going to have fun decorating graham crackers with frosting and making them look like kids in sleeping bags. The kids in the sleeping bags will be you! The only rule in decorating the crackers is that you have to put a smile on your cracker kid's face. You'll find out why later.** Show kids an enlarged copy of the photocopiable diagram on page 17 as a guide for their creations.

After they have finished making their graham cracker sleeping bags, say: **King David was a very important man in the Old Testament. He was very brave. Even when he was a young boy, he showed his bravery by fighting a giant named Goliath. But there were times when even David became scared. There's nothing** wrong with being scared. In fact, we all get scared at times. But David did something when he got scared. Let's find out what it was.

Have each person find a partner. Give each pair a Bible, and ask them to look up Psalm 63:6 to discover what David did at night when he was scared or couldn't sleep. Also have them look up Psalm 4:8 to discover why David was able to sleep in peace. (It might be helpful to write these Scripture passages on a chalkboard or an easel so the kids can refer to them.)

BRINGIN' IT TO A BOIL

After the kids have discovered what David did, give each pair a piece of paper or index card and a pencil.

Say: **You have two minutes to list reasons people get scared. List as many as you can. Go!**

After two minutes, allow pairs to share their lists. Then read Psalm 4:8 to the group again. Ask:

• **Why do you think you had to put a smile on your camper's face?**

Say: **The smile is because the camper has discovered what David did when he was scared at night. Just like David, when you're scared, you can turn to God for comfort.**

Before we eat our camper snacks, let's ask God to watch over and protect us, especially when we sleep at night.

TURNIN' UP THE HEAT

Tell about a time when you were scared and turned to God for help.

SHARIN' IT WITH SOMEONE

Plan a camp-out or a sleepover with a friend. Before you go to sleep that night, tell your friends about David and what he did during scary times.

Permission to photocopy this handout granted for local church use.
Copyright © Dennis and Lana Jo McLaughlin. Published in *FoodFun™: Devotions for Children's Ministry* by Group Publishing, Inc., P.O. Box 481, Loveland, CO 80539.

Fightin' With Swords of the Spirit and Shields of the Faith

SCRIPTURE

Ephesians
6:13-17

COOK'S EYE VIEW: Kids will make fruit kabobs while learning about the armor of God. Discussion focuses on how the armor of God is important in our lives and how it can provide children with protection.

STUFF 'N' FIXIN'S: Various fruits, such as bananas, apples, melons, grapes, pineapple, and strawberries; a bowl for each kind of fruit; knife; skewers (1 per child); 8 ½x11 sheets of construction paper; markers; and scissors.

GETTIN' READY: Decide which fruits you will use for the swords of the Spirit (or fruit kabobs). Cut fruits into chunks, and put each fruit into its own bowl. Cut the sheets of paper in half lengthwise so each measures 4 ¼x11 inches. Place supplies where children have easy access to them.

MIXIN' 'N' MOVIN'

Give each child a skewer, and have children begin making fruit kabobs using their favorite fruits. Tell them they're making swords of the Spirit. As they work on this project, engage them in a simple discussion by asking what swords are used for, if anyone has ever seen a real sword, what fictional or real characters used swords, and so on. When children have finished making their fruit swords, have them place the swords aside and begin the next activity.

Have kids each make shields of faith by folding the piece of construction paper in half, creasing it at the top, and trimming the open ends to form the point of a shield, as illustrated in the diagram on page 19. Be sure to demonstrate the simple steps of this craft for the kids.

After the kids have all finished cutting their papers, provide markers so they each can decorate their shield with a picture that tells about their faith. This might include such things as a cross, an empty tomb, a picture of Jesus, a picture of their family, and so on.

Again, as children are working, engage them in simple discussion asking them to explain what shields are used for. Once they have completed their shields, have them write out Ephesians 6:16-17 on the inside.

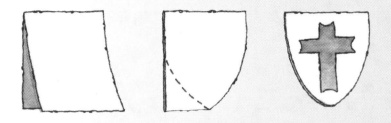

BRINGIN' IT TO A BOIL

Have children form small groups of three to five. Say: **I'm going to assign each group a different person, and I want you to work in your groups and think of ways that person protects us.**

Assign people such as parents, firefighters, police officers, doctors, teachers, and so on. After two or three minutes ask for a report from each group.

Next, read the Scripture passage to the kids, or ask for a volunteer to do it. Ask the following questions, and have the children discuss their answers in their groups:

• **What are ways you believe God protects us?**

• **When was a time you were protected by God? For example, tell about a time when you were sick, in an accident, scared, and so on.**

Have the kids begin eating their Swords of the Spirit as you read aloud verse 17 again, emphasizing the sword of the Spirit as God's word. Ask:

• **What is God's word?**

• **What are ways God's word can protect us?**

• **Why is it so important to study God's word?**

TURNIN' UP THE HEAT

Tell ways Christians can use God's Word like a sword.

SHARIN' IT WITH SOMEONE

Give your shield of faith to someone this week. Tell this person to use it as a Bible bookmark as a reminder of how important it is to study God's word.

Jonah and the Cucumber Whale

SCRIPTURE
Jonah 1:1-3

COOK'S EYE VIEW: In this activity, the kids will make cucumber whales and enjoy eating them with a tasty dip. Plus they'll use the story of Jonah to learn they can't run and hide from what God directs. God expects us to obey him.

STUFF 'N' FIXIN'S: Cucumbers (I for each child plus several more to be cut into slices), I cup creamed cottage cheese, I tablespoon lemon juice, I tablespoon milk, ¼ tablespoon garlic salt, I tablespoon snipped chives, cutting instruments, blender, small bowl, and toothpicks.

GETTIN' READY: Cut the extra cucumbers into slices. Prepare a vegetable dip by placing cottage cheese, lemon juice, milk, and garlic salt into a blender. Blend the ingredients until they are smooth. Pour the mixture into a bowl, stir in the chives and refrigerate for one hour.

The ages of the children in your class will determine how much work you'll have to do on the whales before class. If the children are young, you should do all the cutting and have the kids assemble the cucumber whales. Even if the children are older, be careful about having them use sharp cutting instruments. Often a simple table knife is sharp enough to cut through a cucumber. You can have older kids use table knives to make the cuts themselves. Be sure to have a sharp knife on hand that you can use to assist where necessary. Use the following diagram and instructions to make the cucumber whales.

- Cut a slit in the large end of the cucumber for a mouth.
- Hollow out two eyes and a top air hole.
- Cut thin pieces off the bottom to be placed on the sides of the whale as fins. This also allows the whale to remain flat on the table instead of rolling from side to side.
- Cut slits in the sides to allow the fins to be inserted.
- Cut two pieces off the back to shape the tail.
- While assembling, use toothpicks if necessary to hold the fins in place.

MIXIN' 'N' MOVIN'

Begin by summarizing the story of Jonah. Say: **God told Jonah to tell the people of Nineveh about God. Jonah didn't want to go to Nineveh, so he tried to run and hide from God by sailing away in a boat. But Jonah couldn't get away from God. God caused a fierce storm. Jonah knew the storm was God's way of speaking to him. Jonah ended up being thrown out of the boat and into the sea. Then God sent a large fish, like a whale, to swallow Jonah. While it may not sound like fun to be swallowed by a whale, that was God's way of protecting Jonah. It also gave Jonah time to think about what he'd done wrong. After three days, the large fish spit Jonah out on land. Jonah then went on to Nineveh to tell the people about God. Now we're going to make whales out of cucumbers to remind us how God protected Jonah.**

Have the children assemble their cucumbers according to your instructions. After they have finished, serve the kids a snack of cucumber slices and vegetable dip. Encourage the children to show their cucumber whales to their parents before eating them.

BRINGIN' IT TO A BOIL

As the kids enjoy their vegetable dip snacks, lead a short discussion on the lesson. Begin by reading Jonah 1:1-3 or have a volunteer do it. Ask:

• **Why do you think Jonah tried to run away from God instead of doing what God asked?**
• **What did God do when Jonah disobeyed him?**
• **Why did God protect Jonah in the belly of the fish?**
• **How are people sometimes like Jonah?**
• **What are things God wants us to do that we don't want to do?**

TURNIN' UP THE HEAT

Find a partner, and share something you think God wants you to do but that you're trying to avoid doing.

SHARIN' IT WITH SOMEONE

Identify one person this week who you know God wants you to be friends with but you've been trying to avoid. Make a special effort to become friends with this person.

You Are the Potter

SCRIPTURE
Isaiah 64:8

COOK'S EYE VIEW: Kids will make edible Peanut Butter Modeling Dough and use it to make fun shapes. After having creative fun, they'll enjoy eating the snack as they discuss what it means to be the "work of God's hands."

STUFF 'N' FIXIN'S: (For every 10 children) 1 7-ounce jar marshmallow cream, 1 18-ounce jar smooth peanut butter, 6 tablespoons powdered milk, 6 tablespoons powdered sugar, crushed graham crackers (optional), a large bowl, and photocopies of the "Peanut Butter Modeling Dough" handout (p. 23).

GETTIN' READY: Following the recipe, you can either mix the Peanut Butter Modeling Dough ahead of time or let the kids have a little extra fun and do it themselves. Make sure they all have plenty of room to work around a table. To make the modeling dough extra tasty, sprinkle on crushed graham crackers.

MIXIN' 'N' MOVIN'

Say: **There are several places in the Bible that talk about God being a potter.**

Ask:

• **What's a potter?**

• **What kinds of things do potters make?**

Read Isaiah 64:8 aloud to the class, or have a volunteer do it. Ask:

• **What does it mean that we are the work of God's hand?**

Say: **Today we're going to be potters and make something fun from Peanut Butter Modeling Dough.**

Be sure to have kids wash their hands. Have them begin mixing the ingredients. Then give each child a handful to shape.

Say: **Use your dough to make a shape of something that tells a story about you and God. For example, you could make a heart to represent your love for Jesus, a cross to show that Jesus died for you, or a small person to represent you as one of God's children.**

Encourage kids to be creative. Also, be sure to let them snack on some of the modeling dough as they make their shapes!

BRINGIN' IT TO A BOIL

After everyone has finished, ask each child to tell about his or her shape and what it means. Read the passage from Isaiah out loud again. Let the children enjoy eating their creations while discussing these questions:

- **What were you thinking about when you made your shape?**
- **What do you think God was thinking about when he created you?**

Say: **Just as you are proud of your creation, God is proud of you. God loves every part of his creation—especially each one of you!**

Before the kids leave, be sure to give them each a copy of the Peanut Butter Modeling Dough recipe to take home.

TURNIN' UP THE HEAT

Find a partner, and share one thing that is special about you. Then tell your partner one thing that is special about him or her.

SHARIN' IT WITH SOMEONE

Invite a friend or family member to make some Peanut Butter Modeling Dough with you this week. As you have fun making shapes together, tell him or her how God is the potter and that we're all the works of his hand.

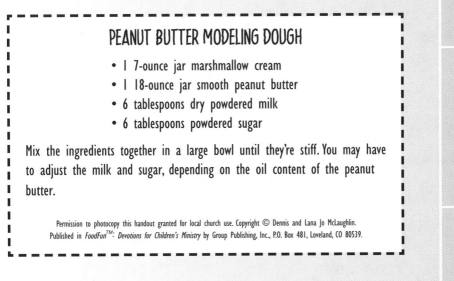

PEANUT BUTTER MODELING DOUGH

- 1 7-ounce jar marshmallow cream
- 1 18-ounce jar smooth peanut butter
- 6 tablespoons dry powdered milk
- 6 tablespoons powdered sugar

Mix the ingredients together in a large bowl until they're stiff. You may have to adjust the milk and sugar, depending on the oil content of the peanut butter.

Permission to photocopy this handout granted for local church use. Copyright © Dennis and Lana Jo McLaughlin. Published in *FoodFun*^{TM}: *Devotions for Children's Ministry* by Group Publishing, Inc., P.O. Box 481, Loveland, CO 80539.

Parable Pumpkin Seeds

SCRIPTURE
Matthew
13:1-8

COOK'S EYE VIEW: The kids will clean pumpkins and toast the seeds. Afterward, they'll make seed pictures while learning about the parable of the sower and discussing things that "choke out" their friendship with God.

STUFF 'N' FIXIN'S: 2 or 3 pumpkins; large spoons; bowls; baking sheets; butter; salt; oven; other kinds of seeds, such as sunflower, poppy, sesame, and so on; various colors of construction paper; scissors; markers; and glue. You'll also need plenty of newspaper or other material to cover the ground or tables where children are scooping out the pumpkins.

GETTIN' READY: Before class, cut the tops off the pumpkins so the kids can clean the seeds out of them.

MIXIN' 'N' MOVIN'

Have kids clean the seeds out of the pumpkins and put them into bowls. When children have finished, allow them to clean their hands. Have an adult wash the seeds well and place them on buttered baking sheets. Lightly salt the seeds, and then roast them in a 350-degree oven for ten minutes.

As you are waiting for the seeds to roast, read aloud Jesus' parable of the sower (Matthew 13:1-8). Review by asking these questions:

- **What are the four types of soil onto which the seeds fell?**
- **What happened to the seeds in each of these situations?**

Say: **Let's make a picture about this parable.**

Have kids gather around a workstation where all the necessary supplies have been placed. Explain that they can cut different colors of construction paper to represent each of the four kinds of soil or use various colors of markers instead. When they've finished this part, have children glue seeds onto their pictures. The pumpkin seeds should be finished and cooled by now. Allow the kids to snack on the pumpkin seeds as they glue the other seeds onto their pictures.

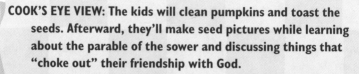

BRINGIN' IT TO A BOIL

Leave the leftover seeds out as you come together for a short discussion.

Say: **After telling the parable of the seeds and the sower, Jesus explained to his friends that the story was about the way people respond when they hear about God.**

Ask:

• **Some seeds fell on hard soil, and birds ate them before they could grow. What kind of situation could this describe?**

• **Some seeds fell on rocky ground. What kind of situation could this describe?**

• **Some seeds fell on thorny or weedy soil. What kind of situation could this describe?**

• **Some seeds fell on good soil. What kind of situation could this describe?**

Have everyone find a partner and discuss the following:

• **Name things in your life that you might let choke out your relationship (or friendship) with God.**

• **Choose which soil you think best tells where your relationship with God is right now. Explain your answer.**

• **A sower is someone who plants seeds. God wants us all to be sowers of his Word. What are ways we can do that?**

TURNIN' UP THE HEAT

Share things you can do in your life right now to plant your relationship with God in good soil.

SHARIN' IT WITH SOMEONE

Think of one way you can be a sower this week and share God's Word with someone. You can do it either by telling that person about your own relationship with God or by doing something kind and unexpected for him or her.

Buildin' a Sweet Temple to God

SCRIPTURE
I Chronicles
29:2-3

COOK'S EYE VIEW: Using bricks of ice cream and bars of chocolate, kids will build a temple, as King Solomon did. Afterwards, they will enjoy a tasty treat while learning about giving their very best to God.

STUFF 'N' FIXIN'S: 2 half-gallon rectangular boxes of ice cream, 4 8-ounce plain chocolate bars, ice-cream cones (1 for each child), 12 x 14-inch board, aluminum foil, plastic gloves, ice-cream scoop, sharp knife, and freezer.

GETTIN' READY: Keep the ice cream in the freezer until just before you are ready to cut it. It is also important to keep the ice cream cold while you build the temple, so you might have to put it back into the freezer for a time during the construction phase.

Cover the board with aluminum foil. Place all the ingredients on a table that allows the kids plenty of room to work. Use the following diagram for reference as you instruct the kids how to build the temple.

MIXIN' 'N' MOVIN'

Say: **In the Old Testament, people didn't have churches to worship in as we do today. Instead, they had a Temple where they went to worship and learn about God. Today, we're going to make a Temple out of ice cream and chocolate bars. But before we do, you should hear a little more about the Temple. Listen as I read a Bible passage about it.**

Read 1 Chronicles 29:2-3 to the kids. Then ask:

• **What did King David give for the Temple to be built?**

26

- **Do you think David gave the very best of what he had for God's temple to be built, or did he give away only the things he didn't need?**

Say: **Since King David gave the very best of what he had for God's temple to be built, we'll do our very best to build the ice-cream temple.**

Ask the kids to gather around the table. Have them put on plastic gloves. Assign each one a specific task. You'll probably want to cut the ice cream bricks yourself. Then have the kids follow your instructions for building the temple.

Cut both blocks of ice cream in half. Leave three of them as they are, and cut the fourth in half again. Have the kids stand three of the blocks next to each other on the foil-covered board to form the major part of the temple. Have them place the smaller pieces on either side of the building to form wings.

Let the kids break the chocolate bars into rectangular pieces, but leave one bar whole. Press the rectangular pieces into the ice cream along the top of the main building as well as the wings. Cut the remaining chocolate bar in half for the door. Press the door into place, and press the remaining rectangular pieces into the ice cream as windows. When the temple is complete, the children may discard their gloves.

Keep the ice cream temple frozen solid until you are ready to serve it. Then serve the kids each a scoop of the tasty temple on ice-cream cones, and add some chocolate pieces on top.

BRINGIN' IT TO A BOIL

Have each of the kids find a partner and share the following:

- **Name three things you own that you wouldn't want to give away to anyone.**
- **Why do you think David gave away some of his best possessions to build a Temple to God?**

After a few minutes, call everyone back together and say: **Giving our best to God doesn't mean giving just things or possessions. It means giving our best service to him also.**

Ask:

- **What are some other ways we can give our best and do our best for God?**

TURNIN' UP THE HEAT

The most important thing in King David's life was serving God. Name the one thing in your life that you spend the most time thinking about and doing. What is something you can begin doing right now to make God more important in your life?

Edible John the Baptist Puppets

SCRIPTURE
Mark 1:4-6

COOK'S EYE VIEW: Kids will make edible John the Baptist puppets while learning about forgiveness and confessing sins.

STUFF 'N' FIXIN'S: Carrots, cucumbers, celery, or potatoes; fresh green beans; cream cheese; raisins; celery; parsley; bean sprouts; wooden craft sticks (1 for each child); cutting knife; bowls; toothpicks; and plastic knives.

GETTIN' READY: Peel the carrots and cut off both ends. Make a cut in the large end of the bottom of the carrots so a craft stick can later be inserted as a handle. Cut the green beans in half. Place all the ingredients into bowls, and place them on a table where kids will have plenty of room to work.

MIXIN' 'N' MOVIN'

Say: **Today we're going to make John the Baptist puppets.**

Ask kids to share what they already know about John the Baptist. Then read Mark 1:4-6 out loud. Ask:

• **What seems to be unusual about John the Baptist?**

• **Have you ever seen or heard of a preacher like John the Baptist?**

• **What was he preaching about?**

Say: **We'll learn more about these things later, but first let's make our John the Baptist puppets.**

Use a carrot for the body, and insert a craft stick in the bottom for a handle. Using cream cheese as glue, stick on raisins for the eyes and nose, a celery slice for the mouth, and parsley for hair. Use the bean sprouts for a beard and for a camel's hair coat. For arms and legs, attach the green beans with plenty of cream cheese. (You may need to use toothpicks to help hold on the arms and legs.)

BRINGIN' IT TO A BOIL

Read the Scripture passage to the kids again. Ask:

• **Why were the people of Jerusalem coming out to see John the Baptist?**

• **What were they doing before John baptized them?**

• **To whom were they confessing their sins?**

• **What does it mean to confess our sins?**

Say: **When we confess our sins, God promises to forgive us. Forgiving means that God will completely erase our sins out of our lives.**

To reinforce this passage, have the kids create a simple puppet show with their puppets. Assign a child to be John the Baptist and a few others to be the people coming to confess their sins. Let the children perform the puppet show for the others from behind a table, holding the puppets above the edge. To add depth to the puppet show, act as an interviewer, and ask the people of Jerusalem what it was like to be forgiven for their sins.

After the puppet show, let the kids enjoy eating their puppets.

TURNIN' UP THE HEAT

Tell about a time when you were forgiven for something by a parent or a friend. How did it feel before you were forgiven? afterward?

SHARIN' IT WITH SOMEONE

Tonight in your prayers, ask God to forgive you for something you haven't yet asked to be forgiven for. Then think of a friend or family member who has done something to hurt your feelings, and forgive him or her for it.

Pharoah's Fruit Chariots

SCRIPTURE
Exodus
14:21-28

COOK'S EYE VIEW: As the kids make edible fruit chariots, they will learn about God's care.

STUFF 'N' FIXIN'S: (For every two participants) 1 banana and 4 strawberries, 1 8-ounce package cream cheese, 1 cup brown sugar, 1 teaspoon vanilla, toothpicks, spoons, cutting knife, and bowls. (As an alternative, you can use celery and carrots in place of the strawberries and bananas and your favorite vegetable dip in place of the cream cheese and brown sugar dip.)

GETTIN' READY: Cut the bananas in half and trim off the ends, but leave the peels on. Slice and trim the strawberries to make circular wheels. Prepare the dip by letting the cream cheese come to room temperature, then mixing it with the brown sugar and vanilla. Assemble a chariot ahead of time to show the kids how a finished one should look.

MIXIN' 'N' MOVIN'

Read Exodus 14:21-28 to the class, or summarize the story about how God parted the Red Sea. Be sure to emphasize how Pharaoh's charioteers were chasing God's people.

Give each student half a banana. Demonstrate how to take the peel off and hollow the banana out with a spoon. After they've hollowed out the main part of their chariots, have the kids attach four strawberry wheels with toothpicks. (Refer to the following illustration as an example of how the chariots should look once they are complete.)

BRINGIN' IT TO A BOIL

After the kids have finished making their fruit chariots, have them gather for a discussion. Ask:

• **If you were crossing the desert and saw an army chasing you, what would you do?**

- **What did Moses do when he saw Pharoah's army coming?**

Have kids form groups of five or six. Ask:

- **If you were in a difficult situation, as God's people in this Bible passage were , would you be more likely to run and hide or more likely to stop and ask God for help?**
- **Tell about a time God helped you out of a difficult situation.**

After a few minutes, say: **When the charioteers were chasing them, Moses and God's people thought there would be no way to escape, but the Lord opened a path through the sea. Whenever we find ourselves in a tough situation, remember that God can open up a way for us to get out.**

Ask:

- **How are the problems you face each day like the problems Moses and God's people faced?**
- **How can we be sure God will take care of us in our difficult situations?**

Conclude the activity by letting the kids devour the edible fruit chariots as the Red Sea devoured Pharaoh's army.

TURNIN' UP THE HEAT

Find a partner, and share a problem or difficult situation you're facing and how you plan to work it out.

SHARIN' IT WITH SOMEONE

Think of a friend or a family member who is facing a difficult problem. Tell him or her the story about how the charioteers chased God's people and how God saved his people. Let this person know you will pray for him or her, and ask God to help with the situation.

Sweet Jesus Mangers

SCRIPTURE
Luke 2:4-7

COOK'S EYE VIEW: Kids will make edible mangers while they learn how and why Jesus was born and what his birth means to them. This is a great Christmas or advent activity.

STUFF 'N' FIXIN'S: (For every 6 to 8 kids) 2 cups chocolate or butterscotch chips, 3 cups chow mien noodles, ½ cup coconut or crumbled shredded wheat, a microwave oven, bowls, clear plastic wrap, paper towels.

GETTIN' READY: Cover a table with plastic wrap. You'll need a microwave oven nearby.

MIXIN' 'N' MOVIN'

Ask:

• **What do you know about the birth of Jesus?**

Read Luke 2:4-7 aloud; then ask:

• **If you could choose which character you would be in the Christmas story, which one would you choose? Why?**

• **What do you think it was like for Mary to have her baby in a stable and have to lay him in a manger?** (If necessary, explain to your class what a manger is: an animal feeding trough, something to keep hay in.)

Place the chips in a microwave-safe bowl, and melt them in the microwave. Mix the chow mien noodles into the melted chips. Let the mixture cool slightly, but not so much that it hardens.

Place a spoonful of candy-covered noodles on the plastic wrap in front of each child. Have the kids each shape the noodles into a manger, then line the bottom of it with coconut or shredded wheat (straw). Allow the mangers to harden for a few minutes.

BRINGIN' IT TO A BOIL

Have the kids stand. Tell them you are going to ask a question and have them each give their answer by moving to one side of the room.

Say: **If you answer one way, line up on this side of the room.** (Point to which side.) **If you answer the other way, line up on the other side.** (Point to which side.)

Ask:

• **How do you picture the place where Jesus was born? dark, dreary, and smelly? or like a pretty Christmas card?**

Be sure to designate which side of the room goes with which answer. If the groups have more than five or six participants each, have them form smaller groups. Then have them sit and discuss the following questions:

• **Why did you answer as you did? What do you think that night was like?**

• **Why do you think Jesus was born?**

Say: **Even though baby Jesus was placed in a simple manger when he was born, his birth was very important. He later died on a cross for us. He promised to always love us. And he promised that if we love him, he will make a place in heaven for us also.**

As the kids eat their Sweet Jesus Mangers, ask:

• **How can we honor Jesus with our Christmas celebrations?**

TURNIN' UP THE HEAT

Think about how Jesus' birth has made a difference in your life. Share what you think your life would be like without Jesus.

SHARIN' IT WITH SOMEONE

Think of someone who will be very lonely this Christmas. Or think of someone who needs Jesus' love in his or her life. Make a Christmas card for that person and deliver it.

Cinnamon Roll Crosses

SCRIPTURE
Colossians
2:13-14

CHEF'S EYE VIEW: The kids will make cinnamon roll crosses while learning about Jesus' death on the cross and forgiveness of sins.

STUFF 'N' FIXIN'S: Ready-to-bake cinnamon rolls (1 can for every 8 to 10 kids), 1 can of white frosting if the cinnamon rolls don't include it, baking sheets, spray cooking oil, oven, and plastic or table knives.

GETTIN' READY: Place all the ingredients on a table where the kids have plenty of room to work.

MIXIN' 'N' MOVIN'

Say: **Today we're going to make cinnamon roll crosses.**

Have kids gather at the table. Open the cans, and give each child a cinnamon roll. There are two types of ready-to-bake cinnamon rolls: biscuit shaped and rolled. If you are using the rolled type, have the kids unroll them and tear off two pieces to make the cross. If you are using the biscuit type, have the kids tear off two pieces for the cross. The crosses will turn out better if the kids twist the dough pieces before baking them.

After the crosses have been shaped, lay them on a greased baking sheet, and follow the baking directions on the side of the can. After you remove the cinnamon roll crosses from the oven, have the kids spread frosting on top.

BRINGIN' IT TO A BOIL

As the treats are baking in the oven, ask your kids to share all the things they know about the cross.

Say: **Jesus was put to death on a cross. It was very heavy, and he was forced to carry it for a long distance. When he arrived at a place called Golgotha, the guards nailed his hands and feet to the cross.**

Ask:

• **What is the heaviest thing you've ever had to carry?**

• **What do you think it would be like to carry a heavy cross?**

• **What do you think Jesus must have felt like as he carried his heavy cross and knew that he was going to die on it?**

Read Colossians 2:13-14. Say: **Although Jesus had never done anything wrong, God allowed him to die so that the sins of all** those who love him will be forgiven. Jesus must have loved us very much to die on the cross so that our sins would be forgiven.

Ask:
- **Have you ever been forgiven by a family member or a friend?**
- **How did it feel to be forgiven?**

Say: **Although Jesus doesn't want us to sin, he'll always forgive us when we ask him. Whenever we see a cross, like the cinnamon roll crosses we made today, we should remember that God forgives us whenever we ask.**

Pass out the snacks. Say: **Before we eat our crosses, let's bow our heads and each silently think of a sin that we want to ask God to forgive. Quietly thank Jesus for dying on the cross so that we will always be forgiven.**

TURNIN' UP THE HEAT

What happened to Jesus after he died on the cross? If you aren't sure, read about it in John 20:10-18.

SHARIN' IT WITH SOMEONE

Ask whoever buys the groceries in your family to buy a can of ready-to-bake cinnamon rolls. Pick a night this week when you and your family can have fun making cinnamon roll crosses together. As you make them, explain what you learned about forgiveness and Jesus' death on the cross.

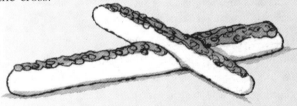

Eatin' Gummies and Fishin' for Men

SCRIPTURE
Mark
1:16-20

COOK'S EYE VIEW: Kids will enjoy eating a lake of gummy fish-filled gelatin, will learn what it means to be fishers of men, and will discuss how they can help bring others to Christ.

STUFF 'N' FIXIN'S: Blue fruit-flavored gelatin (1 3-ounce package for every 4 kids), lots of gummy fish (from a local supermarket or candy store), water, ice cubes, clear plastic parfait cups, pan for boiling, spoons, a fishing pole, and one large plastic fishing bobber.

GETTIN' READY: Prepare the gelatin ahead of time. Stir a 3-ounce package of gelatin into ¾ cup of boiling water. Mix until the powder is dissolved. Next, add enough ice cubes to ½ cup of cold water to make 1 ¼ cups. Add the ice and water to the gelatin, and stir until it begins to thicken. Take out any remaining ice cubes, and pour the gelatin into the parfait cups. Add the gummy fish. Refrigerate the gelatin for approximately 1 to 1 ½ hours, or until it is set.

MIXIN' 'N' MOVIN'

As the kids arrive, pick up the fishing pole, and act as though you're admiring and playing around with it for a few minutes. (You'll probably get a few curious inquiries.) Ask the kids if they like to fish. Have some of them share their favorite fishing stories. Then ask:

• **What's the most frustrating or difficult thing about fishing for you?**

After giving everyone an opportunity to share, tell the group you know an interesting fishing story that comes from the Bible. Read Mark 1:16-20 aloud, or ask for a volunteer to do it.

BRINGIN' IT TO A BOIL

After reading the passage, ask:

• **Why do you think these fishermen followed Jesus?**

Have the kids stand and form their group into the shape of a fish. Hand one child the plastic fishing bobber.

Say: **Take turns tossing the bobber to each other. Whenever you catch it, name one thing that makes Jesus special to you.**

Have the kids remain in their fish shape and sit on the floor. Hand out the gummy gelatin snacks, and let kids begin eating while you continue the discussion. Read the Scripture passage again, and ask:

• **What did Jesus mean when he said, "I will make you fishers of men"?**

Say: **Jesus wants us to be fishers of men also.**

Ask:

• **What kinds of things can we do to help lead or bring other people closer to Jesus?**

TURNIN' UP THE HEAT

Find a partner, and talk about a time when you were a "fisher of men" and did something that might have helped someone come closer to Jesus.

SHARIN' IT WITH SOMEONE

Think of a family member or a friend at school you would like to help come closer to Jesus. Pray for him or her during the week, and think of a way you can be a fisher of men.

Givin' Carrots
Cheerfully

SCRIPTURE

2 Corinthians 9:7 and Leviticus 27:30

COOK'S EYE VIEW: The kids will use "carrot coins" to learn about cheerful giving and be introduced to the concept of tithing. Afterward, they will share a healthy snack of fresh vegetables.

STUFF 'N' FIXIN'S: Several carrots, index cards, and pens or pencils.

GETTIN' READY: Before the class begins, cut the carrots into round, coin-shaped pieces, allowing at least ten coins per child. (For older children, you can create other denominations of coins by using "cucumber coins," "kiwi coins," or any other fruit or vegetable you choose.)

MIXIN' 'N' MOVIN'

As the kids arrive, give each one ten carrot coins, an index card, and a pen or pencil.

Say: **Let's pretend that each carrot coin is worth one dollar. Working by yourself, write on your card how you would spend the money if it were real.**

After two or three minutes have the kids find partners and share their spending plan. As they remain with their partners, say: **Together you have twenty coins to spend. Each coin is now worth ten dollars, so each pair now has two hundred dollars. Decide how you would spend the money together if it were real, and write your plan on the back of your index card.**

After two or three minutes, ask each pair to share their spending decisions with the rest of the class. If any of the pairs say they will give a portion of their money to the church, a worthy cause, or some other work of God's kingdom, ask them to tell why they chose to give a portion in this way. Ask the others to share why they did not choose to give a portion of their money in this manner.

BRINGIN' IT TO A BOIL

Read 2 Corinthians 9:7 aloud and ask:

- **What do you think the Bible means when it says God loves a cheerful giver?**

- **Why is it important to give money to God or to those whose job is to serve God?**

Next, read Leviticus 27:30 to the kids, or ask for a volunteer to do it. Then ask:

- **Who can explain what the word "tithe" means?** (Tithe means one-tenth.)

Give the kids a short math lesson by asking: **If you had ten dollars worth of carrot coins, how much would a tithe be? if you had one–hundred–dollars worth?**

Have kids place their ten carrot coins on a table to use as a visual aid in understanding the concept of tithing. Instruct kids to count their coins and then take one of them away to represent a tithe. Once kids have a basic idea of what a tithe is, have them each eat five carrot coins and then find a new partner.

Provide each pair with another index card, and have them make a new spending plan using ten carrot coins worth ten dollars each (one hundred dollars total). This time, have them include a tithe for God and explain where they would give it.

After two or three minutes, have each pair join with another pair to make groups of four. Give each group another index card, and ask them to think about and record different ways a church uses the money it receives from offerings. Then have each group share what they've written. Tell children about any other ministries in which your church is involved if no one mentioned them in the group sharing.

TURNIN' UP THE HEAT

Why is it important for you to do your part in cheerfully giving offerings to the work of God's kingdom?

SHARIN' IT WITH SOMEONE

Talk to a family member this week about what you discussed in class. Ask him or her to work with you on a plan to be a cheerful giver. You might want to challenge your whole family to work out a plan together.

Invited to a Wedding Banquet

SCRIPTURE
Matthew
22:1-10

COOK'S EYE VIEW: Kids will take part in a make-believe wedding banquet or reception and enjoy tasty foods, such as nuts, cake, mints, and punch. The kids will learn about Jesus' parable of the wedding banquet and how it relates to people who make other things more important than Jesus.

STUFF 'N' FIXIN'S: Can of mixed nuts; a frosted cake; mints; ice ring (optional); punch from your favorite recipe, or use half a gallon of sherbet and 2 2-liter bottles of Sprite or 7-UP; 3 index cards or pieces of paper; small paper plates; napkins; plastic cups; punch bowl; white tablecloth or paper tablecloth; and wedding decorations, such as crepe paper, white paper wedding bells, flowers; and so on.

GETTIN' READY: Since this activity is a make-believe wedding reception, you can be as creative as you want in your decorations. Gather and prepare whatever food items you think are appropriate. Decorate a table on which to set the cake, punch, nuts, mints and so on. (You can save some money by doing this lesson the day after a wedding at your church and using some of the wedding decorations.) Write or type each of the following questions on a separate card or piece of paper:

How would you feel if you invited people to your wedding, but no one came?

What would you do if you were invited to a good friend's wedding, but you had something more important to do at the same time?

What would you do if a couple you didn't know invited you to their wedding because the friends they invited were too busy to come?

MIXIN' 'N' MOVIN'

Have kids form three groups. Give each group one of the prepared cards, and give them two to three minutes to discuss their responses. Then call everyone together, and have them share their answers.

BRINGIN' IT TO A BOIL

Read or summarize Jesus' parable of the wedding banquet as recorded in Matthew 22:1-10.

Ask:

• **In this story told by Jesus, why didn't the guests who were first invited to the wedding banquet come?**

Say: **In this parable, Jesus said the story of the wedding banquet is like the kingdom of heaven.**

Read verse 2 to the group again. Say: **In his story, Jesus tells us that many people are invited to have a friendship, or relationship, with him, but some people think they have more important things to do.**

Have your class return to their three groups. Ask each group to make a list of things we let get in the way of our friendship with Jesus. After three to four minutes, call the class together, and have them share some of their responses. Then invite them to join the wedding reception you've prepared. Begin with a prayer.

TURNIN' UP THE HEAT

Is your relationship with Jesus like the first group of people who were invited to the wedding banquet but were too busy to come? Or are you more like the last group who were invited and came?

SHARIN' IT WITH SOMEONE

On an index card, write down the one thing that gets in the way of your relationship with your family members or friends. Put it on your dresser as a reminder to do better this week.

More Like Mary or More Like Martha?

SCRIPTURE
Luke
10:38-42

COOK'S EYE VIEW: This activity helps kids learn there's a time for both learning about Jesus and for Christian service. Kids will take turns both in serving snacks to one another and in being served. Afterward, they will discuss the merits of both and try to decide whether they're more like Mary or Martha.

STUFF 'N' FIXIN'S: cookies (or other snack of your choice), punch or juice, small paper plates, paper cups, and two age-appropriate story books about Jesus or two of your favorite Bible stories about him.

GETTIN' READY: Before class begins, mix the drink, if necessary, but don't pour it into the cups. The object of this activity is to have the kids prepare the snacks and serve one another. Place the snack items on an appropriate table in your meeting room. Be prepared to read or tell two short stories about Jesus.

MIXIN' 'N' MOVIN'

Form two groups. Explain that one group is to sit in a circle and listen to you tell a story. The other half of the group is to prepare the snack and serve it to the group sitting and listening. Explain that the ones preparing and serving the snack are not allowed to eat or drink anything while they are serving. Instruct them to place the snacks on individual serving plates and to pour the drink into the cups. They should then serve the kids who are listening to the story. (Depending on the age of your group, you may want to ask another adult or teenager to help assist at the snack table. However, the idea is for the kids to do as much of the serving work as possible.)

After you've finished the story and the listeners have finished their snacks, have the two groups trade places: The group that was serving should now sit and listen to you read or tell the second story while the other group serves them a snack.

BRINGIN' IT TO A BOIL

After both groups have finished their snacks, have them gather for a discussion. Ask:

• **Which did you enjoy most, serving the snack to others or being served while you listened to the Bible story? Why?**

• **Which do you think is more important, to sit and learn about Jesus or to serve others? Why?**

• **Was there ever a time when you felt as though you were doing all the work while someone else just sat and took it easy? If so, tell us about it.**

Next, read the Scripture passage about Martha and Mary (Luke 10:38-42), or have one of the kids read it aloud to the group. Ask:

• **How were these two sisters different?**

• **After hearing the Bible story about Martha and Mary, do you think it's better to serve others or to sit and learn about Jesus?**

• **How did you feel when you just sat and listened to the story while someone else waited on you?**

• **How did you feel when you waited on others who sat and learned about Jesus?**

• **When do you think it would be more important to just sit and learn about Jesus?**

• **When do you think it would be more important to serve others?**

TURNIN' UP THE HEAT

Do you think you are more like Mary, or are you more like Martha? Why?

SHARIN' IT WITH SOMEONE

Think of a way you can help or serve one of your family members today, and plan to do it when you get home.

Sweet Salvation Salad

SCRIPTURE
John
3:16-17

COOK'S EYE VIEW: This devotion involves making Salvation Bracelets out of leather lace and pony beads plus making a Sweet Salvation Salad using the same colors as the bracelets.

STUFF 'N' FIXIN'S: 1 3-ounce package of gelatin in each of the following colors: red, blue, green, yellow, and purple; one package of unflavored gelatin; ¼ cup sugar; ¼ cup evaporated milk; 2 teaspoons vanilla; a 9x13-inch baking pan; water; measuring cup; plates or bowls for serving; spoons; leather lace; pony beads in the following colors: purple, red, blue, white, green, and gold or yellow; and scissors.

GETTIN' READY: To prepare the Sweet Salvation Salad ahead of time, make each of the gelatins separately. To make the red, blue, green, and yellow layers, dissolve 1 small package of gelatin in ¾ cup of boiling water; add ¾ cup of cold water.

To make the white layer, combine ½ cup evaporated milk and 2 teaspoons vanilla. Sprinkle 1 package unflavored gelatin over the top. Mix until dissolved; then add ¼ cup sugar and 1 ½ cups boiling water.

Pour the purple layer into the baking pan. Place the pan in the refrigerator, and allow the gelatin time to set. Add the red, blue, white, green, and yellow layers, in that order, allowing time for each layer to chill and set.

MIXIN' 'N' MOVIN'

Have the kids make Salvation Bracelets. Cut pieces of leather lace long enough to be tied loosely around each child's wrist. Have kids string the beads onto the leather one color at a time. Begin by giving each child a purple bead.

Say: **The purple bead stands for sin in our lives. To sin means to do things that are wrong. We all have sin in our lives.**

Next, give each child a red bead, and say: **The red bead stands for Jesus' blood. Jesus died on the cross so that our sins would be forgiven by God.**

Give each child a blue bead, and say: **The blue bead stands for baptism. Jesus was baptized in the Jordan River by John the Baptist. Being baptized means that we believe in Jesus and want our sins to be washed away.**

Give each child a white bead, and say: **The white bead stands for forgiveness. To be forgiven for our sins, we must admit them to God and say we're sorry. Then we are washed white as snow.**

Give each child a green bead, and say: **The green bead stands for Christian growth. We must continue to grow in our friendship with Jesus, even when we become adults. This means that we must spend time praying and studying the Bible.**

Finally, give each child a gold or yellow bead, and say: **The gold bead stands for eternal life. Eternal life means that even after we die, we will live with God in heaven. All we have to do to get eternal life is to ask Jesus into our hearts and promise to love him.**

BRINGIN' IT TO A BOIL

Read John 3:16-17 to the kids. Say: **The Bible tells us that if we believe in Jesus, we'll have eternal life. God sent his Son into the world so we can be saved from our sins.**

Ask:

• **What do we do that can be called a sin?**

• **What are we supposed to do about our sins?**

• **How does the Bible tell us we can have eternal life and go to heaven?**

• **What do you think it means to believe in Jesus?**

Ask some of the kids to look again at their salvation bracelets and review what each color stands for. (Sin, Jesus' shed blood, baptism, forgiveness, Christian growth, eternal life.) Let the kids enjoy eating the Sweet Salvation Salad. As they do, ask them again to tell what each color stands for.

TURNIN' UP THE HEAT

Explain in your own words why God sent his Son to the world.

SHARIN' IT WITH SOMEONE

Wear your salvation bracelet to school and around home all week. When people ask you about it, explain to them what the color of each bead means.

Treasure Muffins—
Your Word in My Heart

SCRIPTURE
Psalm 119:11

COOK'S EYE VIEW: The kids will enjoy a tasty treat while learning about the importance of hiding God's word in their hearts.

STUFF 'N' FIXIN'S: (For approximately 12 muffins) 1 egg, ¾ cup milk, ½ cup applesauce, 2 cups flour, ⅓ cup sugar, 3 teaspoons baking powder, strawberry jam, paper muffin cups, muffin tin, and an oven.

GETTIN' READY: To make muffins, begin by preheating the oven to 400 degrees. Place the paper muffin cups into the muffin tin. Beat the egg, milk, and applesauce together. Stir in the flour, sugar, and baking powder. Fill the muffin cups half full. Spoon one teaspoon strawberry jam into the batter in each cup. Top off with enough batter to fill the cups about three-fourths full. Bake for 20 minutes.

MIXIN' AND MOVIN'

Say: **You've probably all heard stories about hidden treasures.**
Ask:
- **If you could receive any kind of treasure, what would it be?**
- **If you received a valuable treasure, where would you hide it?**

Next, let the kids enjoy eating their snacks.

BRINGIN' IT TO A BOIL

After they've finished eating, ask:

• **Why do you think the muffins are called Treasure Muffins?**

Say: **I want to read you a Bible passage about another hidden treasure.**

Read Psalm 119:11. Ask:

• **According to this Bible verse, where is the treasure hidden?**

• **What is hidden in your heart?**

Say: **When we talk about God's word, we mean the Bible. The words in the Bible are God's words and his message to us. The Bible tells us about things like God's love and forgiveness. It also tells us about things we should do as Christians.**

Ask:

• **How were the Treasure Muffins like God's word?**

• **How can we hide God's word in our hearts?**

• **Why is it important to keep God's word hidden in our hearts?**

TURNIN' UP THE HEAT

Tell about your favorite Bible story and why it's important enough for you to keep it hidden in your heart.

SHARIN' IT WITH SOMEONE

During the next meal with your family, ask family members to tell about a favorite Bible story they've hidden in their hearts.

What's in a Name?

SCRIPTURE
Isaiah 9:6

COOK'S EYE VIEW: The kids will use food coloring mixed with milk to paint various names of Jesus onto bread. Then kids will make toast and see that the names remain. In the process, they will learn more about Jesus and why he is often called by so many different names.

STUFF 'N' FIXIN'S: Milk, food coloring, white bread, cotton swabs, jelly (or other topping of your choice), muffin cups, plastic knives, plates, a toaster, a white board or chalkboard, a marker, and white or light-colored paper.

GETTIN' READY: Fill muffin cups with about one-fourth cup of milk, and add food coloring to them, making a variety of colors. Set all the other items on a table where the kids will have plenty of room to work.

MIXIN' AND MOVIN'

Begin by reading aloud Isaiah 9:6. Ask:

• **Who was the prophet Isaiah talking about?**

Say: **I'm going to read the Bible passage again. As I do, pay special attention to the different names Isaiah calls Jesus.**

Reread the passage. Ask:

• **What names did Isaiah call Jesus?**

Say: **Jesus was called by many names in the Bible. Usually the names that were given to him described things about Jesus. For example, Isaiah described Jesus as wonderful, mighty, everlasting, and he called him a prince. Notice that each one of these says something about who Jesus is.**

Have the kids gather and sit in a circle. Say: **I want us to each take a turn sharing one word about who Jesus is to us.**

As the kids share their words, write each one on the white board. (Be sure to include such words as "cool," "awesome," and any other appropriate descriptive words the kids might use.) Add the following names to the list if they aren't already there. Say: **These are other names given to Jesus in the Bible.**

• **Son of God**
• **Bread of Life**
• **Light of the World**
• **Lamb of God**

- **Good Shepherd**
- **The Truth**
- **Creator**

BRINGIN' IT TO A BOIL

Have the kids gather around the snack table. Say: **Choose your favorite name for Jesus from the list, or think of another one. Dip a cotton swab in the colored milk to write the name on a piece of bread. After you've finished, we'll toast the bread and see what happens.**

Toast the bread, and let the kids see how the names show up even more clearly after the bread is lightly toasted. Let the kids enjoy their snacks by adding jelly or another topping if they choose. After the snack, ask the students each to share the name they used and why they chose it.

TURNIN' UP THE HEAT

Have the kids choose partners. Ask them each to tell their partner a story about Jesus or about something he's done in their lives. Based on that story, have them come up with a name that best describes Jesus.

SHARIN' IT WITH SOMEONE

When you get home, have extra fun by asking all the people in your family to share as many names that describe Jesus as they can think of. Make a list of the names. Write the names on a construction-paper bookmark, and give it to someone special.

The Sweet Taste of Obeyin' God

SCRIPTURE
Genesis
6:11-14;
17-22

COOK'S EYE VIEW: Kids will choose between sweet but plain cookies and colorful but tasteless ones. Then they'll learn about Noah's decision to follow God's command, even though it wasn't easy and may not have made sense at the time. But the result was sweet, just as our decisions are when we obey God.

STUFF 'N' FIXIN'S:

(For 3 dozen sweet cookies) 1 ¾ cups flour, 1 ¼ teaspoons baking powder, ¼ teaspoon salt, ⅓ cup butter or margarine, ¾ cups granulated sugar, ¾ teaspoon vanilla, 1 egg, ½ tablespoon milk, mixing bowls, measuring cups and spoons, a mixer, foil or plastic wrap, a rolling pin, cookie cutters, baking sheets, and an oven.

(For 3 dozen unsweetened cookies) same ingredients as sweet cookies, omitting the sugar; (for frosting) ½ stick of butter or margarine and food coloring.

GETTIN' READY: Make the two types of cookies ahead of time. To make sugar cookies, mix flour, baking powder, and salt. In a separate bowl, cream the butter, add sugar gradually, and beat until fluffy. Add vanilla and eggs. Add flour mixture and milk alternately. Wrap dough in foil or plastic, and chill for several hours. Roll out part of the dough ⅛-inch thick on lightly floured surface. Cut with round 2 ½ inch cookie cutters. Bake on ungreased baking sheets at 400 degrees for eight to nine minutes until the edges are lightly brown. (You can save time on preparing the tasty cookies by using refrigerated cookie dough.)

Make the tasteless cookies the same way. You'll want to make them as appealing as possible by putting "frosting" on them and by adding anything else that will make them delightfully tempting without sweetening them.

To make tasteless frosting, use a hand blender to whip butter or margarine until fluffy. Color with food coloring. Spread frosting on the tasteless cookies after they have cooled. Put the cookies on separate serving plates so the kids can choose between them.

MIXIN' AND MOVIN'

Have each child choose a cookie to eat. Allow them to make their choices without any knowledge of the ingredients. The kids who choose the brightly-decorated cookies will undoubtedly have some interesting comments. Allow the class a few minutes to make their discovery. Then allow the kids who chose a tasteless cookie to eat one of the sweet ones. (If there are tasteless cookies left over, crumble them and use them to feed birds outside.)

BRINGIN' IT TO A BOIL

Ask:

- **What's the difference between the two kinds of cookies?**
- **Why do you think the tasty-looking cookies are so bad, while the plain cookies are so good?**

Ask for a quick show of hands from the kids who know the story of Noah and the ark. Read Genesis 6:11-14. Say: **Noah must have thought it strange that God told him to build an ark when it wasn't even raining. Building a large boat was very hard work and took a lot of time.** Ask:

- **What would have happened to Noah and his family if he hadn't done as God instructed?**

Continue the story by reading Genesis 6:17-22. Say: **The story of Noah and his family ends happily. It rained for forty days and nights, and the whole world flooded. But Noah and his family were saved because he did what God asked, even though it may have seemed hard at the time.** Ask:

- **How was Noah's choice to obey God like the choice of cookies we had a few minutes ago?**
- **Why is important for us to do what God tells us to do, even if isn't easy?**
- **How can we discover what God wants us to do?**

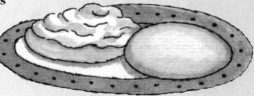

TURNIN' UP THE HEAT

Share a memory about when you did something God wanted you to do and you were glad you chose to do the right thing.

SHARIN' IT WITH SOMEONE

Think of something you haven't been doing at home, but that you know you should be doing. Do it this week, even if it doesn't seem like much fun at the time. This might include such things as being nice to a brother or sister, cleaning your room, doing your homework without being asked, or studying your Bible.

Peelin' Sin and Creatin' Pure Hearts

SCRIPTURE

Psalm 51:2, 10; Romans 6:6-7

COOK'S EYE VIEW: Using a simple apple peeler/corer, the kids will learn what it means to have God create a new heart within them. Our sin is peeled away much as the peeler removes the apple peel. The kids will then enjoy eating apples dipped in fruit dip.

STUFF 'N' FIXIN'S: Apples (1 per child plus a few extra), apple peeler/corer, 2-liter bottle of a carbonated citrus beverage, 8 ounces of cream cheese (at room temperature), ¾ cup powdered sugar, 2 teaspoons orange juice, apple peeler/corer, cutting knife, spoon, bowl for the dip, small serving plates, large punch bowl, pencils, and index cards.

GETTIN' READY: Prepare the fruit dip ahead of time by mixing the cream cheese, powdered sugar, and orange juice in a serving bowl. Pour the citrus beverage into a large punch bowl. Place the dip and punch on a table.

MIXIN' AND MOVIN'

Begin by demonstrating how an apple peeler removes the skin from an apple. Since an apple peeler is safe and relatively easy to use, ask a couple of the kids to try removing the skin from an apple. At this point you're just demonstrating, so tell the rest of the kids they'll get a turn in a few minutes. To keep the peeled items from turning brown too quickly, place them in the bowl of citrus beverage.

Say: **I'm going to read you a Bible verse about a time when David prayed to God.**

Read Psalm 51:2, 10.

Say: **When we use the word sin, we're talking about doing wrong things that aren't pleasing to God. All of us sin. David had done things that weren't pleasing to God, so in his prayer he asked God to clean him from his sins.**

Instruct everyone to find share partners, and give each pair a pencil and an index card.

Say: **Take three or four minutes to think about the kinds of things people do that aren't pleasing to God. Each time you think of a different sin, write it on your index card.**

Call everyone together, and have each pair share its list.

BRINGIN' IT TO A BOIL

Read Romans 6:6-7 to the kids. Say: **The Bible tells us that whenever we sin or do something that is not pleasing to God, like the things we put on our lists, it's possible for us to be forgiven. All we have to do to be forgiven is to ask God to forgive us, as David did. Then God will make us clean again.**

Ask:

• **How is peeling the skin off apples like what God does with our sin?**

• **After God peels away, or removes, our sin, in what ways are our hearts like a newly peeled apple?**

Let the kids gather around the table and finish peeling the apples. Remind them that just as they removed the peel from the apples, God removes our sins when we ask for forgiveness. As the kids take turns with this activity, slice the apples, and let everyone enjoy eating them with the fruit dip.

TURNIN' UP THE HEAT

Cut one apple lengthwise and another crosswise. How do the seeds look different in each one? The apples are the same, but we are looking at them from a different perspective. How does God look at us before our sins are forgiven? How does God look at us after our sins are forgiven?

SHARIN' IT WITH SOMEONE

Tell a family member about the fun way you peeled apples, and how peeling applies is like God forgiving our sins.

Life—a Mixture of Apples and Onions

SCRIPTURE:
Matthew
20:1-16

COOK'S EYE VIEW: Through a snack of good-tasting and bad-tasting foods, kids will learn that life doesn't always seem fair. Afterward, the kids can all share in eating the fresh fruit together.

STUFF 'N' FIXIN'S: A variety of fruits, such as plums, apples, oranges, and peaches; a few onions and bell peppers; a cutting knife; a large basket or container; and aluminum foil.

GETTIN' READY: Before kids arrive, cut and wrap pieces of fruit, onions, and bell peppers in foil so none of the food shows through. About half the packages should contain fruit and the other half, vegetables. Place them all in a basket or other container.

MIXIN' AND MOVIN'

Have each child pick a package from the container. As the children begin opening their packages, explain that this is their snack for the day. However, kids should not begin eating their food yet. You'll probably receive some interesting comments from the kids who open the onions and bell peppers. After they've had a moment to make their discoveries, ask:

• **What seems to be unfair about the snacks this morning?**

Say: **There are many things that happen to us that aren't fair. Share a memory about when something happened to you that seemed unfair.**

BRINGIN' IT TO A BOIL

Say: **Jesus told a story about some workers who thought they weren't being treated fairly. Listen as I read it.**

Read Matthew 20:1-16. Ask:

• **According to this story, what did the landowner do?**

• **What seems unfair about this Bible story told by Jesus?**

• **The workers in the story started to grumble quite a bit. What things could they have done other than grumble?**

• **What would you have said if you had worked all day and received the same pay as someone who had worked only one hour?**

- **Do you think God treats all of us the same? Explain.**

Say: **The end of this story reminds us that God is very generous and we shouldn't be upset when things don't seem fair. People receive different things at different times. God takes care of our needs if we turn to him for help. Maybe the most important thing we can do is be thankful for what we have. One way we can show thanks to God is to share what we have with others.**

Ask:

- **How can those of you who received a piece of tasty fruit show your thanks to God?**

Collect all the fruit, and have the kids enjoy a tasty snack together. Gather the unwanted food items and use them later at home.

TURNIN' UP THE HEAT

How would you answer someone who said to you, "God isn't fair"?

SHARIN' IT WITH SOMEONE

Next time your family shares a meal together, ask if you can say the prayer. Thank God for all he has provided you and your family. Be sure to thank God for your family, friends, and church.

A Land of Milk and Honey—and Maybe a Little Peanut Butter, Too!

SCRIPTURE
Exodus 3:8;
Romans 5:3-4

COOK'S EYE VIEW: Kids will make milk shakes and learn that while God has wonderful promises for the future, there are difficulties along the way. However, God promises that our difficulties can make us stronger.

STUFF 'N' FIXIN'S: (For every 2 children) 1 ½ cups milk, 2 tablespoons chunky peanut butter, 1 tablespoon honey, a blender, a measuring spoon, a measuring cup, and cups.

GETTIN' READY: Place all the items on a table.

MIXIN' AND MOVIN'

Ask:

• If you could go anywhere in the world, where would it be?

• What do you think it would it be like if you could never leave the city where you live, not even for a visit?

Say: **That's exactly what happened to God's people in the Old Testament. They were being held as slaves in Egypt and wanted to leave. But the ruler, a man called Pharaoh, wouldn't allow them to leave. Then God made his people a promise. Listen to it as I read you this Bible passage.**

Read aloud Exodus 3:8. Ask:

• What do you think God meant when he said he would lead them to a land "flowing with milk and honey"?

Say: **After many years, God's people finally arrived in the land of milk and honey. That didn't mean it was a perfect place to live, though. They still had problems. There were still bad people who hurt others. People still suffered with sickness and other difficulties. Some people even chose not to worship God. It was called a land of milk and honey because God promised to go with his people there, to watch over them, and to help them.**

Ask:

• Is there such a place as a land of milk and honey today? If so, where is it?

- **What makes it a land of milk and honey?**

Say: **Today we're going to make milk shakes out of milk and honey, but we are going to add in some chunky peanut butter. There's a good reason for adding peanut butter to the milk and honey. We'll talk about it after we get the milk shakes made.**

Have the kids gather around the table. Let them help you measure the ingredients. Then blend and pour the shakes into cups.

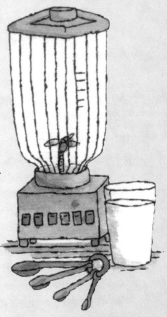

BRINGIN' IT TO A BOIL

Let the kids drink milk shakes as you continue the discussion. Ask if they're able to feel the little chunks of peanut as they drink their milk shakes.

Say: **The milk and honey in our milk shakes represent God watching over us, and the peanut chunks represent the problems we have.**

Ask:

- **How can these milk shakes remind us of our lives?**
- **Why do you think that God sometimes allows us to have problems in our lives?**

Read Romans 5:3-4 to the kids. Say: **God's Word tells us that the problems and difficulties in our lives make us stronger. It also tells us that we should even be thankful for our problems.**

Ask:

- **Since we know that God is with us, what can we do when we have problems?**

TURNIN' UP THE HEAT

Why should we be thankful, even when things go wrong in our lives?

SHARIN' IT WITH SOMEONE

Hold a family meeting, and discuss how each person can help make your home more like a "land of milk and honey."

Lilies of the Field

SCRIPTURE
Matthew
6:27-28

COOK'S EYE VIEW: Kids will enjoy eating tasty flower cookies on a stick while learning about Jesus teaching "not to worry."

STUFF 'N' FIXIN'S: One package of ready-to-bake sugar cookie dough (usually makes 2 dozen cookies), ½ cup solid shortening, ½ cup butter or margarine, 1 teaspoon vanilla, 4 cups powdered sugar, 2 tablespoons milk, yellow food coloring, marshmallows, round candies such as Skittles or M&Ms, craft sticks, scissors, and green ribbon.

GETTIN' READY: Prepare the cookies ahead of time. Prior to baking them, insert a craft stick into each cookie, and then follow the baking instructions on the side of the package. To make the frosting, cream the butter and shortening together. Add vanilla, and then gradually add the sugar, one cup at a time. Add the milk and beat until fluffy. Tint with food coloring.

After the cookies have cooled, spread frosting on them. Using scissors, make flowers for the cookies by cutting a large marshmallow into four pieces for petals. Arrange the petals on each cookie (as illustrated in the diagram), and place a candy in the center. Finish each flower by tying a piece of green ribbon on each craft stick.

MIXIN' AND MOVIN'

Begin this activity by asking these questions:
- **What do you like best about flowers?**
- **What's your favorite kind of flower?**

Say: **We have some cookie flowers to eat as a snack today. They're called Lilies of the Field.** (Hold one up for the kids to see.) **But first let me read you something Jesus said about flowers.**

Read aloud Matthew 6:27-28, and ask:
- **What did Jesus say about flowers in this passage?**
- **Who takes care of flowers?**

BRINGIN' IT TO A BOIL

Let the kids begin eating their Lilies of the Field snacks. Ask:
- **What kinds of things do people worry about?**
- **How can worrying about something make it better?**
- **Why does Jesus tell us not to worry?**
- **How does God care for flowers of the field?**
- **In what ways does God take care of us?**

TURNIN' UP THE HEAT

What are some ways we can learn to worry less and trust God more?

SHARIN' IT WITH SOMEONE

Plan a family walk or hike this week. As you walk together, look around and point out all the ways in which God takes care of his creation.

Sweet Tongues of Fire

SCRIPTURE
Acts 2:1-4

COOK'S EYE VIEW: Kids will construct an edible Pentecost fire and learn about the meaning of Pentecost.

STUFF 'N' FIXIN'S: Stick pretzels, red licorice whips and candy corn.

GETTIN' READY: Place the ingredients on a table where the kids will have plenty of room to work.

MIXIN' AND MOVIN'

Ask:

• What do you like best about birthdays?

Say: **Today we're going to learn about a very special birthday, the birthday of the church. It's called Pentecost.**

Ask:

• If you were in charge of planning a birthday party for the church, what would you include?

Say: **The day the church was born, God sent the Holy Spirit. Jesus had promised to send the Holy Spirit after he had gone to heaven. The Holy Spirit is the presence of God with us. But it came in a very unusual way on Pentecost. Let me read a Bible passage about it.**

Read Acts 2:1-4 to the kids. Ask:

• Where did the violent wind and fire come from?

Say: **God made his presence known to these early Christians in a spectacular way. Since fire was an important part of Pentecost and the coming of the Holy Spirit, we are going to make Sweet Tongues of Fire.**

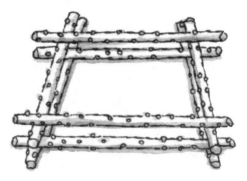

Have the kids gather around the table. Show them how to use eight to twelve pretzels each and put them across one another as in the diagram on page 60.

Next, have the kids break off three-inch pieces of licorice and lay them across the pretzels like flames. Finish the fires by putting two or three pieces of candy corn inside the stacked pretzels.

BRINGIN' IT TO A BOIL

As the kids enjoy eating their Sweet Tongues of Fire, ask:
- **If you had seen the coming of the Holy Spirit at Pentecost, what would you have thought about it?**
- **What does it mean to be filled with the Holy Spirit?**
- **What would a person who was filled with the Holy Spirit do?**

TURNIN' UP THE HEAT

When people are excited about doing something for God, they use the expression, "I was on fire!" Tell about a time when your heart was on fire for God. Maybe it was a time when you did something special for him.

SHARIN' IT WITH SOMEONE

Think of a family member or friend who needs the Holy Spirit in his or her life. Spend time this week praying for that person.

Bread From Heaven

SCRIPTURE
Exodus 16:2-4

COOK'S EYE VIEW: The kids will be like the Israelites who went out to search for and gather bread from heaven. Kids will understand that God provides for their needs and will also get to sample different and unusual kinds of bread. This activity requires either multiple rooms or a large activity room, such as a gym. (Or it can be played outside.)

STUFF 'N' FIXIN'S: 6 to 8 different types of bread, such as wheat, white, pumpernickel, rye, sourdough, French, raisin, cinnamon, multigrain, tortillas, pita, poppy-seed, banana, or rice cakes; a large resealable plastic bag for each bread; and one small sandwich bag for each person.

GETTIN' READY: Cut the loaves into one-inch chunks, and place each type into its own resealable bag. Before the kids arrive, hide the containers of bread (much as you would hide Easter eggs.) Be sure to place the containers far enough apart that the kids will have to spend a few minutes gathering up a piece of each bread sample.

MIXIN' 'N' MOVIN'

Give each child a sandwich bag.

Say: **Today we're going to play a mystery search game. We'll be searching for bread. The object is to find each hidden container, take one piece of bread from it, and put it into your sandwich bag. After you take a piece from a container, leave the container where it is hidden, and begin searching for the next one.**

Be sure to tell kids how many different types of bread they're to look for. Instruct them to return to the designated area when they have found all the samples. Also, be sure to discuss your boundaries ahead of time, especially if you have a large search area. Give them a five- to ten-minute time limit, depending on your search area, and have them begin.

After the search is complete, have your group gather and sit in a circle with their bags. Let kids guess what each type of bread is (be sure to let them know the correct answer), and have them begin sampling the rewards of their search. Spend a minute or two allowing them to talk about which breads they like and which they dislike.

Gather up the hidden containers, and let the kids snack on their favorite breads while you lead a discussion.

BRINGIN' IT TO A BOIL

Read or have one of your students read Exodus 16:2-4 aloud. Then ask:

- **Why were the people grumbling to Moses?**
- **Have you ever grumbled about being hungry? Tell us about it.**
- **What happened when the people grumbled about being hungry?**
- **Do you think God would have provided something for the people to eat even if they hadn't grumbled about being hungry? Why or why not?**
- **Next time you're tempted to grumble, what could you do instead?**
- **How does it feel to know God wants to provide for all your needs?**

TURNIN' UP THE HEAT

Would you still be thankful toward God even if you had only bread to eat every day for a whole year? Why or why not?

SHARIN' IT WITH SOMEONE

Think of someone who provides for you and thank them today!

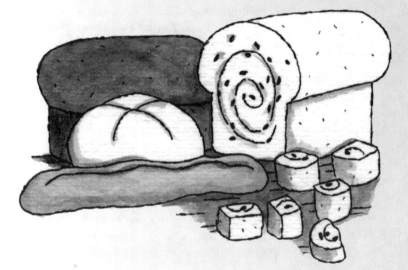

Never Give Up—on Ice Cream

SCRIPTURE
Galatians 6:9

COOK'S EYE VIEW: Kids will make homemade ice cream in coffee cans and learn the importance of not giving up and eventually reaping the reward.

STUFF 'N' FIXIN'S: (For every 4 kids) 1 1-pound coffee can with plastic lid, 1 3-pound coffee can with plastic lid, 1 cup cream, ¾ cup milk, 1 egg, 1 teaspoon vanilla, ½ cup sugar, crushed ice, rock salt, serving bowls, spoons, an ice-cream dipper, a measuring cup, measuring spoons, a wrist watch, and duct tape.

GETTIN' READY: Place everything on a table where the kids can combine the ingredients. Find an outside area with plenty of room. Mark start and finish lines for a noncompetitive kick-the-can relay.

MIXIN' 'N' MOVIN'

Explain that today everyone will be making homemade ice cream as well as playing a fun game. Have kids form teams of four. Guide the teams in combining the ingredients for ice cream.

Say: **Mix the following ingredients into your small coffee can: one cup of cream, three-fourths cup of milk, 1 egg (break the yoke up), 1 teaspoon of vanilla, and a half cup of sugar.**

Next, put the lid on your can, and use duct tape to seal it tightly. Place the small can inside the larger can. Pack the large can with a half-cup of rock salt and as much ice as possible. Put the lid on the large can, and seal securely with duct tape.

You may want to help put the tape on to make sure it's secure. The keys to success in this activity are (1) seal the lids securely, (2) do not overfill the cans, and (3) pack in plenty of ice and salt.

Next, have all the kids move to the relay area, and instruct the teams to line up at the starting line.

Say: **The object of this game is to move your can from the start line to the finish line and then back again. It's not a race, and you're not competing against anyone. You'll push or gently roll the can with your hands or feet. After the first person in line completes one round, he or she is to hand the can off to the next person in line. You'll have to do this for twenty-five minutes—which is a long time, so don't wear yourselves out by running too fast. The most important rule comes from Galatians 6:9.**

Read it to the group, and then let them begin.

If the kids become weary of going back and forth, let them form a small circle and roll the can back and forth. Continue motivating the kids to keep the can moving, even if they become bored or tired. Perseverance is an important part of the lesson. After the time is up, open the cans, and serve ice cream to the kids.

BRINGIN' IT TO A BOIL

As the kids eat their well-deserved portion of ice cream, ask:
- **What were you thinking as you were playing this game?**
- **What would have happened if you had given up?**
- **What happened because you didn't give up?**

Read Galatians 6:9 again. Ask:
- **How was playing the ice cream game like the message in this verse?**

Say: **God's word challenges us not to become discouraged. We're to keep on doing good and trust God for the results. If we do, in time we'll receive the reward, just as we did with the ice cream.**

Ask:
- **If we do what God asks, what reward will we receive?**
- **What'll happen if we get tired of doing something and give up on it before we have a chance to finish it?**
- **What things does God expect us to do even though we might become tired of doing them?**

TURNIN' UP THE HEAT

Think of something you would like to accomplish but think it will take too much time and work. What would the Bible say about it? If you aren't sure, read Galatians 6:9.

SHARIN' IT WITH SOMEONE

Think of a person, either in your family or at school, that you have a hard time being friends with. Spend some extra time this week trying to get along with that person. Remember, God's Word promises that in the end it will be worth it!

Wise and Foolish Builders

SCRIPTURE

Matthew
7:24-27

COOK'S EYE VIEW: Kids will build houses out of crackers with various "glues" and see which ones can stand through a storm. As they enjoy peanut butter and crackers, the kids will learn that Jesus is a lot like the "glue" in our lives.

STUFF 'N' FIXIN'S: Full-sized saltine crackers, peanut butter, whipped cream, table knives, and a plate for each child. (If you are concerned that children in your group may be allergic to peanuts, use canned frosting instead of peanut butter throughout this activity.)

GETTIN' READY: Prepare two tables by putting the whipped cream on one, the peanut butter on the other, and the crackers, plates, and knives on both.

MIXIN' 'N' MOVIN'

Have kids form two groups. Assign Group A to the table with whipped cream and Group B to the table with peanut butter.

Say: **The object of this game is to build a house on your plate using the ingredients on the table. You can build the house however you want—just be creative. To hold the crackers together, you can use the whipped cream or the peanut butter, whichever is on your table. I'll give you about ten minutes to finish. You may begin.**

BRINGIN' IT TO A BOIL

When the kids have finished their houses, ask:

• **Which houses do you think are the strongest, the ones made of peanut butter or the ones made of whipped cream? Why?**

Say: **I'm going to pretend I'm a storm and shake the houses you built to see which ones stand and which ones fall.**

Have the kids assemble at the peanut butter table. Gently shake the houses, which should resist falling down because of the peanut butter. Next, move to the other table, and gently shake the houses made of whipped cream. These should fall apart fairly easily because of the whipped cream.

Read aloud Matthew 7:24-27, and ask:

• **How were the houses you made out of whipped cream and crackers like this Bible verse?**

• **How were the houses you made out of peanut butter and crackers like the Bible verse?**

• **In Jesus' story, why didn't the house made of stone fall down when the storm came?**

• **What kind of people did Jesus say were the ones who built their house on a rock?**

• **How is Jesus like the peanut butter we used in house building game?**

Say: **The houses in Jesus' story are like our lives. If we listen to Jesus' words and do as he asks, our lives will be as strong as a rock. If we don't listen to his words and don't do what he asks, our lives will be like a house built on sand.**

As the kids enjoy eating a snack of peanut butter and the crackers from their house, have each of them find a partner. Give the pairs two to three minutes to answer the following questions:

• **What can we do to make sure our lives are strong and built upon a rock?**

• **What do people do that make their lives like a house built on sand?**

Have the pairs share a few of their thoughts after they have had adequate time for discussion.

Say: **To make our lives strong, like the houses we made out of peanut butter, we must learn God's word and obey it. Even if things become difficult in our lives, we can remain strong because we know we're doing what Jesus wants.**

TURNIN' UP THE HEAT

Name something you do that makes your life "unsteady," like the house built of sand. Name something you do that makes your life like one built on a rock.

SHARIN' IT WITH SOMEONE

Think of a family member or friend who seems to be building his or her life on sand. Pray that he or she will begin listening to and obeying the words of Jesus.

Hidden Treasures and Seekin' After God

SCRIPTURE:
Matthew
13:44-46

COOK'S EYE VIEW: This activity involves a hide-and-seek game and a treasure to help kids understand Jesus' parables of the hidden treasure and the pearl.

STUFF 'N' FIXIN'S: White yogurt-covered raisins; clear plastic wrap; plastic sandwich bags (one for each child); and a whistle, bell, or other signal device.

GETTIN' READY: Wrap small handfuls of raisins in clear plastic wrap. Hide the yogurt-covered raisin packets around a room as you would hide Easter eggs. (Since yogurt-covered raisins melt easily, it's best not to hide them outside on a warm day.) Make sure you hide enough to serve as the kids' snacks.

MIXIN' 'N' MOVIN'

Say: **Let me tell you a story. There once was a little girl who was playing hide-and-seek with her sisters. While she was hiding, the others decided not to play anymore and went inside without telling her. She got upset and began to cry. When her mother came out to see what was wrong, the little girl told her what had happened.**

Ask:

• **How do you think this little girl felt when she discovered no one was looking for her?**

• **What do you think the mother should have said to the little girl?**

• **How do you think God must feel when we get too busy doing other things and don't take time to pray or think about him or read our Bibles?**

Give the kids each a plastic sandwich bag.

Say: **We're going to play a game. It's a search game. I've hidden packages of candy that looks like pearls. When I say go, you have three minutes to look for the pearls. When you find a package, put it into your bag and keep looking. When I blow the whistle, report back to this location. Ready, go!** (If necessary, be sure to give them boundaries before you send them out.)

BRINGIN' IT TO A BOIL

After the kids have returned from their search, allow them to begin eating their snack as you read them Matthew 13:44-46. Then say: **This Bible passage tells us that the kingdom of heaven, or being with God, is more valuable than anything else we can have or find.**

Ask:

- **What did the man do who found the pearl of great value?**
- **How is this pearl of great value like God?**
- **How was our searching for pearls like what we should do with God?**

TURNIN' UP THE HEAT

Name one thing you're going to do to make God the most valuable treasure in your life.

SHARIN' IT WITH SOMEONE

Play hide-and-seek with family members or friends. Be sure to play it the right way. After the game, tell them the story about the little girl and how God must feel when we don't go in search of him.

More Than Milk

SCRIPTURE

Hebrews
5:13-14

COOK'S EYE VIEW: This activity begins as a fun game where pairs search their Bibles for clues to discover the ingredients for a treat that is much more than milk. As they enjoy their snacks, they'll learn about Christian growth by comparing it to a baby growing old enough to move from milk to solid food.

STUFF 'N' FIXIN'S: (For every 3 to 4 kids) 2 cups milk, ⅓ cup frozen grape juice concentrate, and 2 scoops vanilla ice cream; a blender; a measuring cup; an ice-cream scoop; cups; Bibles; pencils; and copies of the "More Than Milk Clue Sheet" handout on page 71. (Be sure to keep the snack ingredients out of sight until after the kids have uncovered their clues.)

GETTIN' READY: Make copies of the handout. If your kids are too young to locate the Bible passages themselves, you may want to write the passages on index cards.

MIXIN' 'N' MOVIN'

Say: **Today we're going to make a snack called More Than Milk. But I'm not going to tell you what the snack is. You'll have to discover that yourself by looking for clues in the Bible. Everyone find a partner to work on the clue sheet with. When you've discovered what the snack is made of, yell, "More than milk!" and bring your handout to me. After everyone has finished, we'll make the snack.**

As the kids find their partners, hand each pair a Bible, a copy of the handout and a pencil.

After the kids have all discovered the ingredients, have them help you create the treat. Blend the milk, the frozen grape juice concentrate, and the vanilla ice cream until smooth. Pour into cups and serve.

BRINGIN' IT TO A BOIL

Begin a discussion by asking these questions:
• **What kind of food do young babies live on?**
• **Why can't babies live on milk forever?**
• **What would happen to a baby who never had anything more than milk to drink?**

Say: **The Bible tells us our relationship (or friendship) with God is like a baby who at first drinks milk and later eats solid foods.**

Read aloud Hebrews 5:13-14. Ask:

• **What are the two types of people these verses talk about?**

Say: **The Bible says solid food is for the mature. To mature means to grow.**

Ask:

• **What things can we do to grow in our relationship with God?**

• **How is growing as a Christian like a baby growing up?**

TURNIN' UP THE HEAT

Share something in your life that you can do to show you're a Christian who eats "more than milk."

SHARIN' IT WITH SOMEONE

One way to show we're mature Christians is to do helpful things for others. When you get home today, think of a way you can serve one of your family members.

MORE THAN MILK CLUE SHEET

When you discover each clue, write it in the space on the bottom of the handout.

CLUE 1: Look up 1 Corinthians 3:2. Paul said I gave you _____, not solid food.

CLUE 2: Look up Luke 6:44 to discover what people don't pick from briers.

CLUE 3: Look up Job 6:15-16 to see what makes the streams dark.

Ingredients for More Than Milk

CLUE 1: _____

CLUE 2: _____ juice

CLUE 3: _____ cream

Be sure to yell, "More than milk!" when you've discovered all the ingredients.

Permission to photocopy this handout granted for local church use. Copyright © Dennis and Lana Jo McLaughlin. Published in *FoodFun!™: Devotions for Children's Ministry* by Group Publishing, Inc., P.O. Box 481, Loveland, CO 80539.

The Shepherd and His Sheep

SCRIPTURE
John 10:3-5, 14-16

COOK'S EYE VIEW: Kids will make sheep out of marshmallows and coconut, play a game trying to recognize various people's voices, and better understand how they can recognize the voice of Jesus.

STUFF 'N' FIXIN'S: One bag large marshmallows, one bag small marshmallows, shredded coconut, several small bowls, plastic knives, scissors, sweet paste made of 1 ½ tablespoons milk and 1 cup powdered sugar, tape recorder, blank tape.

GETTIN' READY: Make a tape recording of several different unidentified but recognizable voices. Include voices such as the pastor, some of the kids' parents, a popular television star, a teenager in the church, the president of the U.S. (from television or radio address) and so on—be creative. Each voice recording should be about five seconds long. Next, make the sweet paste by mixing milk and powdered sugar in a bowl. Put the paste and shredded coconut (separately) into smaller bowls. Use scissors to snip marshmallows into ears. (See diagram.) Place all the ingredients on a table where the kids will have plenty of room to work.

MIXIN' 'N' MOVIN'

Say: **Tell me what you know about sheep.** (After waiting a moment for responses, continue.) **The Bible tell us a shepherd "calls his own sheep by name and leads them...and his sheep follow him because they know his voice. But they will never follow a stranger... because they do not recognize a stranger's voice"** (John 10:3-5).

Ask:

• **How do we recognize a person's voice?**

• **Why is it important to be able to recognize the voice of people we're close to, like our parents, the pastor, or our teachers?**

Say: **I'm going to play a tape recording of some voices. See if you** can guess who they are. If you recognize a voice, don't say the name. Raise your hand, and I'll call on someone to give the answer.

Begin the game by playing the recording of each voice. Pause after each one to let the kids guess whose voice it is.

After the game, say: **We are going to continue learning about Jesus and sheep by listening to a Bible passage and then making some sheep out of marshmallows.**

Read aloud John 10:14-16. Ask:

• **Who's the good shepherd?**

• **Who are the sheep?**

Have the kids gather and make marshmallow sheep according to the illustration. It will be easier for the kids if you demonstrate.

Say: **Use a plastic knife to spread sweet paste on the end of a marshmallow. Stick another marshmallow to it to make the body. Use large marshmallows for the sheep's body and head. Then attach small marshmallows as feet and a tail. For ears, paste on the snipped marshmallows. After your sheep is together, spread sweet paste on it, and sprinkle it with coconut.**

BRINGIN' IT TO A BOIL

When kids have finished making their sheep, say: **Sheep who don't recognize the voice of their shepherd don't know who to listen to and follow.**

As the children enjoy their snacks, ask:

• **What are some reasons a sheep might not recognize the voice of his shepherd?**

• **How's our relationship with Jesus like the relationship between a shepherd and his sheep?**

• **What does it mean for us to recognize Jesus' voice?**

Say: **Those who don't spend time getting to know Jesus have a difficult time knowing what he want us to do.**

Ask:

• **What are some things we can do to get to know Jesus better?**

TURNIN' UP THE HEAT

Why is it hard to know the difference between what's right and wrong if we don't recognize Jesus' voice?

SHARIN' IT WITH SOMEONE

Ask your mom or dad to buy a copy of the book *Fun Excuses to Talk About God* by Joani Schultz. Plan for your family to spend time using the book to talk about Jesus so you can learn to easily recognize his voice.

Plagued by Frog-Eye Salad

SCRIPTURE

Exodus 8:1-4,
9:8-10, 22-24,
10:21-22

COOK'S EYE VIEW: The kids will experience some of the plagues God sent against the Egyptian Pharaoh when he refused to listen. Kids will learn that they must turn their attention to God.

STUFF 'N' FIXIN'S: 1 cup sugar, ½ teaspoon salt, 1 ¾ cup pineapple juice, 2 tablespoons flour, 3 egg yolks, 1 cup acini di pepe pasta, 1 large can crushed pineapple, 1 package miniature marshmallows, 1 9 ¾-ounce container of nondairy whipped topping, green food coloring, 1 bag of birdseed, 1 package of red-hot candies, mixing bowl, serving bowls, and plastic spoons.

GETTIN' READY: Prepare Frog-Eye Salad at least two days prior to this activity. Combine sugar, salt, pineapple juice, flour, and egg yolks in a bowl. Cook and stir over low heat until thick. Cook pasta; drain and cool. In a mixing bowl, combine the pasta with sugar mixture, and refrigerate overnight. The next day, add the crushed pineapple (drained well), the marshmallows, and the nondairy whipped topping. Mix well and tint with food coloring. Refrigerate the salad until just before you are ready to serve it.

MIXIN' 'N' MOVIN'

Say: **There was a time when God's people were being held as slaves by a king called Pharaoh in the country of Egypt. God wanted Moses to lead the people away from Egypt into a beautiful new land. Moses went to Pharaoh and asked him to let God's people go. But Pharaoh refused. To demonstrate his power and convince Pharaoh to let the people go God sent ten plagues, or times of great trouble, on the Egyptians. We're going to have fun experiencing four of the plagues, even though they weren't any fun in real life.**

Read Exodus 9:8-10 aloud. Hand out some red-hot candies to each of the kids, and say: **First, we'll experience what it might be like to have boils, or sores, all over our bodies. Lick a few pieces of your candy, and stick them on your arms, hands, and face.**

Allow the kids a few minutes to accomplish this. Have them look at each other and themselves. Ask:

• **What do you think these boils must have felt like to the Egyptians?**

• **If you were Pharaoh and boils broke out all over your body, would you let God's people go? Why or why not?**

Allow the kids time to remove the candies and wash off the sticky spots. Wet wipes would work well. Next, take the kids outside, and have them stand in a line with their eyes closed. Read Exodus 9:22-24 to them. Then throw handfuls of birdseed on them and have them imagine it's hail. Ask:

- **How do you think real hail felt as it rained down?**
- **Why is hail so damaging and dangerous?**
- **If you were Pharaoh and hail fell on everyone throughout the land, would you let God's people go? Why or why not?**

Next, read Exodus 10:21-22 to the kids. Take them into a darkened room. If you are unable to darken the room completely, have the kids close their eyes. Ask:

- **Would you be afraid if there was no light for several days? How would you feel?**
- **If you were Pharaoh and darkness covered all Egypt for three days, would you let God's people go? Why or why not?**

Return to your regular meeting area. Read Exodus 8:1-4 aloud.

Say: **We can't exactly experience a whole country covered with frogs. But I've made some Frog-Eye Salad for you to eat.**

Serve the snack to the kids. (Assure them that the salad is sweet and tasty. The little pasta pieces are not really frogs' eyes!) As the kids are eating it, ask:

- **If you were in a place covered with frogs, what do you think it would be like?**
- **If you were Pharaoh and frogs covered the whole country, would you let God's people go? Why or why not?**

BRINGIN' IT TO A BOIL

Say: **Eventually the mean Pharaoh did let God's people go, but only after God sent ten plagues.**

Ask:

- **Why do you think Pharaoh was so stubborn?**
- **What is it about the plagues that makes you know that God loves his people?**
- **Share some ways that you know God loves you.**

TURNIN' UP THE HEAT

Talk about something in your life you know God wants you to do but that you're being stubborn about and not doing.

SHARIN' IT WITH SOMEONE

Tell one of your family members or friends how God sent the plagues on Pharaoh and the Egyptians to help the people he loved. Assure the person you are talking to that God loves them in the same way.

New Creation Lemonade

SCRIPTURE
2 Corinthians
5:17

COOK'S EYE VIEW: Kids will add cabbage-juice ice cubes to yellow lemonade. The lemonade will change color without changing its taste. This activity helps kids understand how Christ changes us into new creations.

STUFF 'N' FIXIN'S: I head of red cabbage, water, cutting knife, pan, stove, strainer, ice cube trays, frozen yellow lemonade concentrate, pitcher, cups.

GETTIN' READY: Prepare the ice cubes prior to this activity. Chop a head of red cabbage, and put it into a pan. Add just enough water to cover and simmer for approximately twenty minutes. Let the cabbage cool, and strain the juice into ice cube trays. (The liquid will be blue.) Freeze into ice cubes. Mix the frozen lemonade concentrate in the pitcher.

MIXIN' 'N' MOVIN'

Say: **Things change almost everyday. For example, each day we get older; each day new babies are born; each day some people die. The seasons change, from spring to summer, from fall to winter, then back to spring again. Changes happen inside people also. For example, people's feelings change from sad to happy and from bravery to fear.**

Ask:

• **What things can make people's feelings change?**

• **What are changes that have happened recently in your life?**

Say: **The Bible tells us that when we ask Jesus into our hearts, our lives change.**

Read 2 Corinthians 5:17 to the kids. Say: **We're going to try an experiment to see how this works. I've made special ice-cubes. After I pour a cup of lemonade for each of you, add one or two ice cubes and watch what happens.**

Pour the lemonade for the kids, and then allow a few minutes for them to observe how it turns from yellow to pink after the ice cubes have been added.

BRINGIN' IT TO A BOIL

As the kids drink their lemonade, read the Bible passage to them again. Ask:

- **How is what the ice cubes did to the lemonade like what Jesus can do to our lives?**
- **How can a person be changed into a new creation?**
- **When Jesus changes our lives, what kinds of things are different for us?**
- **What did the Bible passage mean when it said, "the old has gone, the new has come"?**
- **Since those who ask Jesus into their hearts are different on the inside, how should they treat others?**

TURNIN' UP THE HEAT

Share something that has changed since Jesus came into your life.

SHARIN' IT WITH SOMEONE

Since those who have been changed into new creations by Jesus are supposed to treat others differently, think of something extra special you can do today for everyone in your family.

Findin' Room for God

SCRIPTURE
Matthew 6:33

COOK'S EYE VIEW: The kids will discover the importance of putting God first by demonstrating how quickly other things can fill up our lives

STUFF 'N' FIXIN'S: I quart jar with a lid, 3 walnuts or large jaw-breakers (or any other item about the same size), enough popcorn kernels to fill the jar after putting the walnuts in, microwave popcorn, a large bowl, and small paper cups.

GETTIN' READY: Pop the microwave popcorn ahead of time to serve as a snack. To prepare the experiment, place three walnuts in the bottom of a quart jar. Next, fill the jar to its rim with popcorn kernels. Put the lid on, and shake the jar to make sure all the popcorn settles. Take off the lid, and fill to the rim again if the popcorn has settled. Take the walnuts out and keep them separate for the experiment while leaving the exact amount of popcorn in the jar. You will discover that when you put the popcorn in first, the walnuts won't fit on top and allow the lid to go on.

MIXIN' 'N' MOVIN'

Have kids gather around so they can all participate in the experiment. Pour equal amounts of the popcorn kernels from the jar into paper cups, one for each child. Place the walnuts beside the jar.

Read Matthew 6:33 to the kids. Say: **Even though God wants us to put him first in our lives, we often let other things become more important. We're going to do an experiment to see what happens when we let other things become more important than God. As we do this experiment, we'll let these walnuts represent God. We'll let the popcorn kernels in your cups represent all the things we often make more important than God. Think of something you do during the daytime; it can be anything from brushing your teeth to playing with your friends.**

Have the kids take turns naming an activity they often do during the day. As each one shares, have that child pour his or her cup of popcorn kernels into the jar. When everyone has finished, put the walnuts on top, and show the kids that the lid won't go on the jar.

Say: **When we're busy doing other things during the day and don't allow God to be first in our lives, there's not enough room**

left for God. But let's see what happens when we put God in first.

Start again by removing the walnuts and pouring the popcorn into the children's cups. This time, place the walnuts into the jar first. Have the kids take turns naming another of their daily activities and again pouring their cups of popcorn into the jar. When they have finished, demonstrate how the lid clearly fits onto the jar.

BRINGIN' IT TO A BOIL

Let the kids fill their cups with popped popcorn and begin snacking as you talk about the experiment. Ask:

• **How was putting the walnuts into the jar first like putting God first in our lives?**

• **How was putting the walnuts into the jar last like making other things in our lives more important in our lives than God?**

• **Why is it important to put God first in our lives?**

• **What are ways we can put God first in our lives?**

TURNIN' UP THE HEAT

Name something you sometimes let become more important than God each day. How can you show that God is the most important thing in your life?

SHARIN' IT WITH SOMEONE

Talk to your family about making sure you start every meal with a prayer. Also, suggest that you pray as a family before going on trips together.

Born of Water and the Spirit

SCRIPTURE
John 3:1-7

COOK'S EYE VIEW: Kids will have "tasty" fun with this experiment where they first taste plain soda water and later add a white grape juice and create a delicious bubbly drink. This activity, coupled with the story of Nicodemus, teaches kids what it means to be "born of water and the Spirit."

STUFF 'N' FIXIN'S: Bottles of soda water, white grape juice, and cups.

GETTIN' READY: Place all the ingredients on a table that the kids can gather around.

MIXIN' 'N' MOVIN'

Ask:

• What are the differences between a newborn baby and someone your age?

Say: **It's easy to see the differences between newborn babies and those who are older. But there are other things you can't tell about people just by looking at them.**

Ask:

• When you look at someone, how can you tell whether he or she is good or bad?

Say: **In the same way, you can't really tell if a person is a Christian just by looking at his or her appearance. In the Bible, there was a man named Nicodemus who didn't understand one of Jesus' stories because he was thinking about a person's outside appearance only. Listen as I read the story to you.**

Read aloud John 3:1-7. Ask:

• **What did Nicodemus think Jesus meant when he talked about a man being "born again"?**

Say: **Jesus was talking about the inside of a person. Jesus meant that our souls, or the part of us that makes us who we are, are "born again" when we receive the Holy Spirit. Let's do an experiment to demonstrate how this works.**

Let's let this water represent a person who doesn't know about God.

Pour about one-third cup of soda water for each child, and have them take a small drink. Ask:

• **What does the water taste like?**

• **How are people who don't have God in their hearts like this water?**

Say: **Let's let this white grape juice represent the Holy Spirit.**

Mix about as much juice in the kid's cups as they have water, and have them taste it.

Say: **The sweet juice helps the drink taste much better and sweeter. Even though it looks the same as it did before, the drink is different on the inside. That's why Nicodemus didn't under-stand about what it meant for a man to be "born again." He was thinking about the outside of a person and not the inside.**

BRINGIN' IT TO A BOIL

As the kids finish their drinks, ask:

• **How is being "born again" like what we did to the plain water?**

• **Why can't we tell by looking at another person if he or she has received the Holy Spirit and been "born again"?**

• **What things does a person who has been "born again" do?**

• **How would you define "born again" in your own words?**

• **How can a person receive the Holy Spirit and be "born again"?**

TURNIN' UP THE HEAT

Can people tell by looking at you that you have the Holy Spirit in your heart? If they watch you for several days, what would they be able to learn about you? How are your actions and attitudes different from those of a person who isn't a Christian?

SHARIN' IT WITH SOMEONE

Look for people showing they have the Holy Spirit in their hearts. As you see them doing kind things for you or others, be sure to thank them.

Sweet and Sour Protection

SCRIPTURE

Psalm
121: 7-8

COOK'S EYE VIEW: Kids will observe how apple slices coated in lemon juice don't turn brown as the uncoated ones do. The lemon juice protecting the apples will provide a lesson about God's watchful protection.

STUFF 'N' FIXIN'S: 8 ounces cream cheese, ¾ cup brown sugar, 1 teaspoon vanilla, several apples, slicing knife or apple peeler, bowl, bottle of lemon juice, and small serving plates.

GETTIN' READY: Prepare the fruit dip ahead of time. Allow the cream cheese to come to room temperature. Mix the brown sugar and vanilla into the cream cheese. Place the dip in a serving bowl.

Peel and slice one apple just before the class begins. Sprinkle lemon juice on half the slices. Place the apples on a plate so the uncoated pieces will begin turning brown. Put all the ingredients on a table.

MIXIN' 'N' MOVIN'

Begin peeling an apple. As you do, ask:

• **What happens to a peeled apple if you let it sit out for a while?**

Have the kids gather around the table. Show them the brown slices of apple you peeled just before class.

Say: **When we take the peel off an apple, it's no longer protected from the air. After it sits around in the air for a while, unprotected, it turns brown. In a way, it's like someone going outside in a short-sleeved shirt when the weather is very cold.**

Ask:

• **How is going out in the winter without a coat like peeling the skin off an apple?**

Say: **There's something we can do to protect an apple after it's been peeled. We can sprinkle lemon juice on it.**

Peel and slice several apples, and give each child a few slices on a plate. Pass the lemon juice around, and have the kids each sprinkle some juice on about half their slices. The other half they should leave untreated.

BRINGIN' IT TO A BOIL

While the kids are waiting to see the results of their experiment, have them sit. Read Psalm 121:7-8 aloud. Ask:

- **According to the Bible passage, what will the Lord do?**
- **How is God like the lemon juice we put on the apple slices?**
- **How does it make you feel to know God is always watching over you?**

Give the kids an opportunity to examine the results of their experiments. Let the kids eat the apple slices and the fruit dip.

TURNIN' UP THE HEAT

Share the memory of a time when God protected you from harm.

SHARIN' IT WITH SOMEONE

Think of a family member or friend who is going through an especially rough time. Pray that God will watch over that person's life.

Grace Pudding

SCRIPTURE
Ephesians
2:8-9

COOK'S EYE VIEW: This fun and wet activity will help kids better understand how God's grace works.

STUFF 'N' FIXIN'S: (For every 4 children) 1 3.4-ounce box of instant pudding (any flavor), milk, 4 large bowls; 4 chairs; small paper cups; and water.

GETTIN' READY: Mix pudding according to the instructions on the side of the box, and pour it into small paper cups. Refrigerate until ready to serve.

Position two chairs as the starting line of a relay area, and put a bowl of water on each chair. Place the other two chairs opposite these chairs, about fifty feet away. Place one empty bowl on each of these chairs. (If your group is very large, add two additional chairs and two additional bowls, and set up a third relay group.)

MIXIN' 'N' MOVIN'

Have kids form two teams. Have each team line up behind their starting chair (one with water on it).

Say: **The goal of this game is to see how much water you can get from your bowl at the starting line into the bowl at your finish line. You are allowed to carry the water only in your bare hands. When I say "Go!" scoop up some water in your hands, run to the empty bowl, and pour whatever water is left in your hands into the bowl. Then run back to the starting line so the second person can begin running. We'll keep running until each team has** completely emptied their bowl at the starting line. Then we'll see which team got the most water into their second bowl. Ready? Go!

After this race, measure the amount of water in each bowl, and congratulate the winning team. Then empty two bowls, refill the starting line bowls with fresh water, and give each player a paper cup.

Say: **Let's run the relay again, only this time, rather than carrying the water in our hands, we'll carry it in paper cups. Ready, go!**

Again congratulate the winning team, then gather for discussion.

BRINGIN' IT TO A BOIL

Ask:

• **What happened when you tried to carry the water in your hands?**

• **Why was it easier to carry the water in cups?**

Read Ephesians 2:8-9 to the kids.

Say: **This Bible passage uses the word grace. Grace is a way that God shows his love for us by forgiving us, even though we don't deserve it. This passage lets us understand that we can't get to heaven by doing good things. We can only get to heaven because of God's grace and his love for us.**

Ask:

• **What was it like to carry water in your hands?**

• **How is that like what would happen if we tried to get into heaven by ourselves, without God's grace?**

• **How was the experience of carrying water in cups like having God's grace and love in our lives?**

• **What are some good things that happen in your lives because of God's grace and love?**

Say: **Now I'm going to give you something even better than water in your cups.**

Give the kids their pudding snacks. As they begin eating, ask:

• **How does this pudding remind you of God's grace?**

TURNIN' UP THE HEAT

What would things be like in this world without God's love and grace?

SHARIN' IT WITH SOMEONE

Use a piece of paper and pencil to make a list of all the ways that God shows his love. Be creative! Think of someone who's having a bad day, and give him or her the list as a reminder of God's love.

Secret Christian Pretzels

SCRIPTURE
Matthew
6:1-4

COOK'S EYE VIEW: In the spirit of doing acts of kindness in secret, the kids will make homemade pretzels and deliver them anonymously to others.

STUFF 'N' FIXIN'S: (For 10 medium-sized pretzels) 1 tablespoon yeast; ½ cup warm water; 1 teaspoon honey; 1 teaspoon salt; ⅓ cup flour; 1 egg, slightly beaten; ¼ cup grated cheese (optional); a large mixing bowl; a pastry brush; measuring spoons; measuring cups; plastic gloves; baking sheets; plastic wrap; ribbon; paper or index cards; pencils or pens; and access to an oven.

MEASURIN' & MIXIN': Before class, place the ingredients and utensils on a table so the kids can make the pretzels themselves. Preheat the oven to 425 degrees.

MIXIN' 'N' MOVIN'

Form groups of four. Ask each group to read Matthew 6:1-4 and discuss what they think Jesus was teaching. (If your class is of a younger age, you might want to either write the passage out on an index card for each group or read it aloud to them and have them discuss it in groups.)

Allow up to five minutes for group discussion, and then have everyone come together. Explain to the kids that they are going to make Christian pretzels and deliver them in secret, just as Jesus talks about in the Bible passage.

Have kids gather around the table and put on plastic gloves. Instruct them to follow the instructions as you read.

Say: **Dissolve one tablespoon of yeast in half a cup of warm water. Next, add one teaspoon of honey and one teaspoon of salt. Then add one-third of a cup of flour.** (You can also add a quarter cup grated cheese at this point if you choose.)

Next, demonstrate how to knead the dough, and have kids do this themselves. Then have the kids each shape the dough into snake-like forms, approximately eight inches in length, and bend them into different Christian symbols, such as crosses, fish, circles, and so on. Place the pretzels on the baking sheets, and brush them with egg. Bake the pretzels for ten minutes at 425 degrees. After the pretzels are done, allow them to cool and then wrap them in plastic wrap. Tie three to five pretzels together with the ribbon.

As the pretzels are baking and cooling, hand out sheets of paper or index cards, and have the kids write a special-delivery message on each one without revealing who the pretzels are from. The note might include a favorite Bible verse or a short poem—be creative! Attach a note to each package of Secret Christian Pretzels.

Following the discussion, go out and make your secret deliveries. For extra fun, have the kids secretly sneak the packages onto the front porches of the recipients, ring the doorbell, and then run off. (It may help to have extra drivers, depending on the size of your class and the number of deliveries you plan to make.)

BRINGIN' IT TO A BOIL

While the kids are snacking on the extra pretzels, have them get back into their original groups of four.

Ask:

• **Why do you think Jesus teaches us to do acts of kindness without telling others?**

After a few minutes, read Matthew 6:1-4 out loud.

Say: **It's often good for us to do acts of kindness in secret so we don't call attention to ourselves. It's more important to give credit to God than take credit ourselves.**

Ask:

• **How does it make you feel when you do something kind for another person without telling them?**

TURNIN' UP THE HEAT

Have the kids find a partner and discuss examples of kind things they can do for others without telling them.

SHARIN' IT WITH SOMEONE

When you get home today, do something kind for one of your family members without telling them.

Plantin' And Eatin'

SCRIPTURE
James 2:15-17

COOK'S EYE VIEW: Kids will go to the home of an elderly or shut-in person and help plant flowers. Afterward, they'll share watermelon as a snack and use watermelon seeds as an object lesson to learn about serving others.

STUFF 'N' FIXIN'S: Flower plants, small planting tools, watering can, slices of watermelon containing seeds.

GETTIN' READY: Get permission from an elderly or shut-in person to bring the kids over to his or her house and plant some small flowers. Arrange transportation for the kids. Cut slices of watermelon for a snack. (Be sure to leave the seeds in.)

MIXIN' 'N' MOVIN'

Help (or supervise) the kids as they plant some small flower plants outside the home of an elderly person. Afterward, have them wash their hands and then gather for their watermelon treat.

BRINGIN' IT TO A BOIL

Read James 2:15-17 aloud. Say: **Let's answer the question the Bible asks. Suppose there is someone who needs help. You say, "I hope you find someone to help you," but you go on your way and do nothing about it. How have your helped that person?**

This Bible passage tells us the way to know if someone's Christian faith is real is to look at his or her actions. It means that our Christian faith isn't real if we don't have helpful actions that go along with it.

Ask:

• **What are things we can do to show our Christian faith is real?**

• **How did we show today that our Christian faith is real?**

Say: **Pick up a watermelon seed and look at it for a minute. The seed is very small. Think how big it must grow to become a whole watermelon. Plus, in every watermelon, there are hundreds of seeds just like that one. And each one of those seeds can grow a watermelon with hundreds more seeds again. It is amazing when you think about it.**

Ask:

• **How does a tiny watermelon seed grow into a very large piece of fruit?**

• **How are our helpful Christian actions like watermelon seeds?**

Say: **God provides for us and takes care of us, just as he does a watermelon seed. God asks that we thank him by doing helpful things for others, just as we did today. Every time we do something kind and helpful for someone, our actions are like the watermelon seeds: They bring God great happiness and show our Christian faith is real.**

TURNIN' UP THE HEAT

Name something you can do this week to show that your Christian faith is real.

SHARIN' IT WITH SOMEONE

Get together with your family, and think of a helpful service project you can all do together this week.

Passin' on the Faith

SCRIPTURE
2 Timothy 1:5

COOK'S EYE VIEW: Kids will eat soup as well as make dried soup to be put into jars and delivered to someone who has made a difference in their lives. They'll also discuss how Timothy's faith was passed to him from his mother and grandmother.

STUFF 'N' FIXIN'S: (For each child) ½-quart jar with a lid, 1 ¼ cups instant mashed potatoes, 1 ½ cups nonfat dry milk, 2 tablespoons instant chicken bouillon, 2 teaspoons dried minced onion, 1 ½ teaspoons seasoned salt, 1 teaspoon dried parsley, ¼ teaspoon dried whole thyme, ¼ teaspoon ground white pepper, ⅛ teaspoon turmeric, ¼ cup powdered grated American cheese, measuring cups, measuring spoons, several large bowls, copies of the "Potato Soup Recipe" handout (p. 92), colored ribbon, scissors, pencils, bowls, spoons, and boiling water.

GETTIN' READY: Place all the dry ingredients in bowls so the kids can measure and put together the soup mix. Make copies of the recipe handout (p. 91). Place all the ingredients on a table where the kids have plenty of room to work.

MIXIN' 'N' MOVIN'

Say: **Today we're going to talk about people who've helped us to become better Christians, especially family members. Think about a family member who has helped you with your Christian faith.**

I'm going to read a Bible passage to you. The passage is part of a letter that a man named Paul wrote to his friend Timothy. Paul knew that Timothy was a man with a very deep Christian faith. Listen and see who Paul said was responsible for Timothy's being such a good Christian.

Read aloud 2 Timothy 1:5. Ask:

• **Who did Paul say was responsible for Timothy's Christian faith?**

• **How might Timothy's mother and grandmother have helped him in his Christianity?**

• **Name the family member(s), or others, who have helped you most in your Christian faith.**

Say: **I'm sure Timothy must have been very thankful for his**

mother and grandmother. As a way for us to say thank you to those special people in our lives, we're going to make something for them.

Ask the kids to gather around the table. Using the recipe on the handout, help the kids each put together a jar of dried soup. Be sure to have them stir the ingredients together as they put them in the jars. (Make enough extra soup for the kids to enjoy as a snack after they have finished. Each jar will serve approximately eight to ten people. For serving instructions, see the handout.)

After the kids have finished filling their jars, say: **Be sure the lid to your jar is on tight. Then take one of the handouts, fill in the name of the person you want to give it to, and sign your name. When you're finished, attach it to the neck of your jar by tying it on with a piece of ribbon.** (Be sure to assist those who need it.)

BRINGIN' IT TO A BOIL

Serve warm soup to the kids so they can taste what they're giving as a gift. As the kids are enjoying their soup, ask:

• **Why is it important to have family members and other people in our lives who help us in our Christian faith?**

• **What are ways we can help others learn about Jesus just as Timothy's mother and grandmother helped him?**

TURNIN' UP THE HEAT

Think of a family member or friend who needs help in his or her Christian faith. Share what you can do to help that person's faith grow stronger.

SHARIN' IT WITH SOMEONE

Deliver your jar of soup to someone special!

To: _____ ⭕

Read 2 Timothy 1:5 for a clue as to why you are special in my life. You remind me of Lois and Eunice. This special soup treat is my way of thanking you for helping me become a better Christian.

POTATO SOUP MIX

1 ¼ cups instant mashed potatoes
1 ½ cups nonfat dry milk
2 tablespoons instant chicken bouillon
2 teaspoons dried minced onion
1 ½ teaspoons seasoned salt

1 teaspoon dried parsley
¼ teaspoon dried whole thyme
¼ teaspoon ground white pepper
⅛ teaspoon turmeric
¼ cup powdered grated American cheese

To serve, place ¼ cup soup mix in a bowl or mug. Add 1 cup boiling water and stir until smooth. Let soup sit 1 or 2 minutes to thicken slightly.

From: _____

Permission to photocopy this handout granted for local church use. Copyright © Dennis and Lana Jo McLaughlin. Published in *FoodFun™: Devotions for Children's Ministry* by Group Publishing, Inc., P.O. Box 481, Loveland, CO 80539.

To: _____ ⭕

Read 2 Timothy 1:5 for a clue as to why you are special in my life. You remind me of Lois and Eunice. This special soup treat is my way of thanking you for helping me become a better Christian.

POTATO SOUP MIX

1 ¼ cups instant mashed potatoes
1 ½ cups nonfat dry milk
2 tablespoons instant chicken bouillon
2 teaspoons dried minced onion
1 ½ teaspoons seasoned salt

1 teaspoon dried parsley
¼ teaspoon dried whole thyme
¼ teaspoon ground white pepper
⅛ teaspoon turmeric
¼ cup powdered grated American cheese

To serve, place ¼ cup soup mix in a bowl or mug. Add 1 cup boiling water and stir until smooth. Let soup sit 1 or 2 minutes to thicken slightly.

From: _____

Permission to photocopy this handout granted for local church use. Copyright © Dennis and Lana Jo McLaughlin. Published in *FoodFun™: Devotions for Children's Ministry* by Group Publishing, Inc., P.O. Box 481, Loveland, CO 80539.

Indexes

SCRIPTURE INDEX

SUBJECT INDEX

Group Publishing, Inc.
Attention: Product Development
P.O. Box 481
Loveland, CO 80539
Fax: (970) 679-4370

Evaluation for *FoodFun*™: *Devotions for Children's Ministry*

Please help Group Publishing, Inc., continue to provide innovative and useful resources for ministry. Please take a moment to fill out this evaluation and mail or fax it to us. Thanks!

● ● ●

1. As a whole, this book has been (circle one)

not very helpful   very helpful

1   2   3   4   5   6   7   8   9   10

2. The best things about this book:

3. Ways this book could be improved:

4. Things I will change because of this book:

5. Other books I'd like to see Group publish in the future:

6. Would you be interested in field-testing future Group products and
   giving us your feedback? If so, please fill in the information below:

Name _____

Street Address _____

City _____ State _____ Zip _____

Phone Number _____ Date _____

Permission to photocopy this handout granted for local church use. Copyright © Dennis and Lana Jo McLaughlin. Published in *FoodFun*™: *Devotions for Children's Ministry* by Group Publishing, Inc., P.O. Box 481, Loveland, CO 80539.

BRING THE BIBLE TO LIFE FOR YOUR 1ST- THROUGH 6TH-GRADERS... WITH GROUP'S HANDS-ON BIBLE CURRICULUM™

Energize your kids with Active Learning!

Group's **Hands-On Bible Curriculum**™ will help you teach the Bible in a radical new way. It's based on Active Learning—the same teaching method Jesus used.

In each lesson, students will participate in exciting and memorable learning experiences using fascinating gadgets and gizmos you've not seen with any other curriculum. Your elementary students will discover biblical truths and <u>remember</u> what they learn because they're <u>doing</u> instead of just listening.

You'll save time and money, too!

While students are learning more, you'll be working less—simply follow the quick and easy instructions in the **Teacher Guide**. You'll get tons of material for an energy-packed 35- to 60-minute lesson. And, if you have extra time, there's an arsenal of Bonus Ideas and Time Stuffers to keep kids occupied—and learning! Plus, you'll SAVE BIG over other curriculum programs that require you to buy expensive separate student books—all student handouts in Group's **Hands-On Bible Curriculum** are photocopiable!

In addition to the easy-to-use **Teacher Guide**, you'll get all the essential teaching materials you need in a ready-to-use **Learning Lab**®. No more running from store to store hunting for lesson materials—all the active-learning tools you need to teach 13 exciting Bible lessons to any size class are provided for you in the **Learning Lab**.

Challenging topics each quarter keep your kids coming back!

Group's **Hands-On Bible Curriculum** covers topics that matter to your kids and teaches them the Bible with integrity. Switching topics every month keeps your 1st-through 6th-graders enthused and coming back for more. The full two-year program will help your kids...

- •make God-pleasing decisions,
- •recognize their God-given potential, and
- •seek to grow as Christians.

Take the boredom out of Sunday school, children's church, and midweek meetings for your elementary students. Make your job easier and more rewarding with no-fail lessons that are ready in a flash. Order Group's **Hands-On Bible Curriculum** for your 1st-through 6th-graders today.

Hands-On Bible Curriculum is also available for
Toddlers & 2s, Preschool, and Pre-K and K!

Order today from your local Christian bookstore, or write: Group Publishing, P.O. Box 485, Loveland, CO 80539.